Alfred Hitchcock's *Rear Window*

Alfred Hitchcock's *Rear Window* is one of the icons of American film making. A perfect example of Hollywood cinema at its best, it is an engaging piece of entertainment as well as a fascinating meditation on the nature of the film itself. A suspense thriller about a chair-bound observer who suspects his neighbor of murdering his wife, the narrative becomes the vehicle for Hitchcock's exploration of the basic ingredients of cinema, from voyeurism and dreamlike fantasy to the process of narration itself. This volume provides a fresh analysis of *Rear Window*, which is examined from a variety of perspectives in a series of new essays published here for the first time. Providing an account of the actual production of the film, as well as feminist and cultural readings of it, it also demonstrates the influence of *Rear Window* on a wide range of film makers, including Antonioni, De Palma, and Coppola, among others.

John Belton is professor of English and film at Rutgers University. The author of *American Cinema/American Culture* and *Widescreen Cinema,* which won the Kraszna-Krausz Award for Books on the Moving Image, he is a founding member of the National Film Preservation Board.

THE CAMBRIDGE UNIVERSITY PRESS FILM HANDBOOKS SERIES

General Editor

Andrew Horton, *University of Oklahoma*

Each CAMBRIDGE FILM HANDBOOK is intended to focus on a single film from a variety of theoretical, critical, and contextual perspectives. This "prism" approach is designed to give students and general readers valuable background and insight into the cinematic, artistic, cultural, and sociopolitical importance of individual films by including essays by leading film scholars and critics. Furthermore, these handbooks by their very nature are meant to help the reader better grasp the nature of the critical and theoretical discourse on cinema as an art form, as a visual medium, and as a cultural product. Filmographies and selected bibliographies are added to help the reader go further on his or her own exploration of the film under consideration.

Alfred Hitchcock's
Rear Window

Edited by
JOHN BELTON

CAMBRIDGE
UNIVERSITY PRESS

PUBLISHED BY THE PRESS SYNDICATE OF THE UNIVERSITY OF CAMBRIDGE
The Pitt Building, Trumpington Street, Cambridge, United Kingdom

CAMBRIDGE UNIVERSITY PRESS
The Edinburgh Building, Cambridge CB2 2RU, UK   http://www.cup.cam.ac.uk
40 West 20th Street, New York, NY 10011-4211, USA   http://www.cup.org
10 Stamford Road, Oakleigh, Melbourne 3166, Australia
Ruiz de Alarcón 13, 28014 Madrid, Spain

First published 2000

Typeface Stone Serif 9.75/14 pt. *System*   QuarkXPress® [GH]

*A catalog record for this book is available from
the British Library.*

Library of Congress Cataloging-in-Publication Data

Alfred Hitchcock's Rear Window / edited by John Belton.
        p.   cm. – (Cambridge film handbooks)
     Filmography: p.
     Includes bibliographical references and index.
     ISBN 0-521-56423-9. — ISBN (invalid) 0-521-56453-0 (pb)
     1. Rear window (Motion picture) I. Belton, John. II. Series.
PN1997.R353A43   2000
791.43'72 – dc21   99-12160
                                                          CIP

ISBN 0 521 56423 9 hardback
ISBN 0 521 56453 0 paperback

Transferred to digital printing 2004

To Vivian

Contents

Acknowledgments

I would like to thank Andy Horton for his faith in this project and his patient support in seeing it through. At Cambridge, Beatrice Rehl and Anne Sanow provided professional expertise in the very best, Hawksian sense of the terms. Scott Curtis was extremely helpful in directing me toward material that greatly assisted me in my role as editor. Alan Williams and Jane Belton were wonderfully generous in the time and effort they put into the translation of Michel Chion's essay. For other contributions, direct or indirect, I would also like to thank Arlene Bubrow, Steven DeRosa, Tom Gunning, Tim Hunter, Peter Jaszi, Elisabeth Weis, Susan White, and Robin Wood.

Contributors

John Belton teaches film in the English Department at Rutgers University and is the author of *American Cinema/American Culture* (McGraw-Hill, 1994), *Widescreen Cinema* (Harvard, 1992), and other books.

Michel Chion is an experimental composer, a director of short films, and a critic for *Cahiers du cinema.* He has published numerous books in French on film sound as well as books on screenwriting, Jacques Tati, Charles Chaplin, and David Lynch. His book on David Lynch and two of his books on sound, *Audio-Vision: Sound on Screen* and *Voice in the Cinema,* have recently been translated into English

Scott Curtis, formerly the Special Collections Research Archivist for the Academy of Motion Picture Arts and Sciences' Margaret Herrick Library in Beverly Hills, is now an assistant professor in the Department of Radio/Television/Film at Northwestern University.

Elise Lemire is Assistant Professor of Literature at Purchase College, The State University of New York. She is currently working on a book titled *Making Miscegenation: Discourses of Interracial Sex and Marriage in the U.S., 1790–1865.*

Sarah Street teaches Film and Television Studies in the Department of Drama at the University of Bristol and is the co-author of *Cinema and State: The Film Industry and the British Government* (British Film Institute, 1985). She has previously written on costume in Hitchcock's films for *Hitchcock's Annual, 1995–96*. Her most recent book is *British National Cinema* (Routledge, 1997) and her current research is on the distribution and reception of British films in the United States.

Armond White, former arts editor and film critic for *The City Sun,* has written for *Premiere, The Village Voice, The New York Times, Rolling Stone, The Nation, Essence,* and many other publications. He is the author of *The Resistance: Ten Years of Pop Culture That Shook the World* (New York: The Overlook Press, 1995).

JOHN BELTON

Introduction

SPECTACLE AND NARRATIVE

Like many of the best works of classical Hollywood cinema, *Rear Window* is a deceptively obvious film. Its chief virtues are clearly visible for all to see. An exemplary instance of commercial motion picture entertainment, it represents the best that Hollywood had to offer its audiences in the tumultuous 1950s.[1] (Indeed, its classic status continued to be reaffirmed in the 1990s; in 1997, the Librarian of Congress placed it on the National Film Registry, and in 1998, it was listed among the American Film Institute's best 100 American films of all time.) Filmed in glorious Technicolor and projected on a big screen in a widescreen format,[2] it is, on a purely technological level, a compelling example of 1950s motion picture spectacle. Though its subject matter lacks the epic proportions of that era's big-budget biblical spectacles, costume pictures, or westerns, its basic situation is pure spectacle. Indeed, its story is "about" spectacle; it explores the fascination with looking and the attraction of that which is being looked at. The story goes as follows: Confined to a wheelchair with a broken leg, photojournalist L. B. Jefferies (James Stewart) has little to do but to look out his rear window at his Greenwich Village neighbors. He suspects that one of them, a jewelry salesman named Thorwald, has murdered his invalid wife. With the help of his girlfriend, Lisa Fremont (Grace Kelly), and his nurse, Stella (Thelma Ritter), he continues to observe Thorwald until evidence is discovered that confirms that Thorwald did, indeed, kill his wife.

In a number of ways, the film looks back to what scholars of

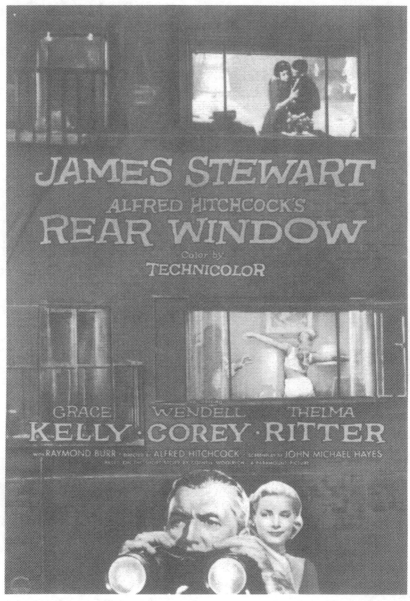

The Cinema of Attractions: An original poster for *Rear Window* exploits its status as spectacle. Note the ad's rearrangement of apartments and rewriting of basic story material (the sinister hand) to emphasize love, sex, and potential violence. Photo courtesy of Paramount.

early cinema have termed "the cinema of attractions."[3] According to Tom Gunning, early (i.e., pre-1906) films were more concerned with exhibition, presentation, and display than with narration. They consisted of a series of loosely connected acts or attractions, resembling, in part, the structure of a vaudeville show. Though *Rear Window* has a strong narrative line and is centrally concerned with the act of narration, its story is grounded not only in voyeurism but also in exhibitionist display, "revealing [as its advertising copy proclaims] the privacy of a dozen lives."[4] It consists of a "montage of attractions," of various windows that display a variety of different "acts." The film is about what the hero sees out his rear window. What he sees is apparently random – different neighbors are engaged in various, unrelated activities. These activities constitute the film's spectacle. The sense that the hero makes out of these activities comprises the film's narrative, a narrative that he imposes, as it were, on seemingly random events.

Rear Window is spectacle in more traditional ways as well. It is concerned with the display of its lavish set and costumes. The film's set (discussed in this volume by Scott Curtis) remains one of its chief attractions; it is a "star" in its own right, dominating posters and other advertising material for the film on its initial release. "Fifty men worked for two months to build the set, which includes seven apartment buildings, most of them six stories high, and three smaller buildings on the other side of the street."[5] Occupying an entire sound stage, the set measured 98 feet in width, 185 feet in length, and 40 feet in height; it cost more than $9,000 to design and more than $72,000 to construct. These were unprecedented costs for a single studio set in 1954.

Designed by Edith Head, the costumes worn by the film's heroine (also discussed elsewhere by Sarah Street) represent the latest in Paris fashion. The display of these costumes provides the viewer with a kind of fashion show, a form of spectacle that was a staple of Hollywood productions of the past (from *Fifty Years of Paris Fashions, 1859–1909*, 1910, to *Cover Girl*, 1944, *Singin' in the Rain*, 1952, and *Funny Face*, 1957) and that continues into the nineties (*Ready to Wear*, 1994). Popular awareness of costume design in motion pictures was longstanding, but critical interest in the "art" of costume design blossomed only a few years before *Rear Window;* the first Academy Award for Costume Design was presented as recently as 1948. Fashion featured in the headlines in 1947, when Christian Dior unveiled his "New Look" in Paris. Interest in fashion dramatically escalated in the 1950s when Oleg Cassini, Dior, and Givenchy became household names. At the same time, fashion magazines, such as *Harper's Bazaar* (the journal read by the heroine in the film's last scene), functioned as mass-produced fashion shows in pictures and print and brought the spectacle of fashion to millions of postwar, middle-class, female consumers.

On a purely visual level, then, *Rear Window*'s set and costume design provide viewers with something spectacular to look at. The film's story and theme build on this highly visible base, exploiting and exploring the nature of spectacle. The film does this by examining more abstract aspects of the relationship between spectator and spectacle, between the film's voyeur-hero and what he sees. It addresses the concepts of voyeurism and exhibitionism and explores the nature of their interconnectedness.

The film is deceptively obvious in that it is, above all, so eminently entertaining. It combines an engagingly suspenseful murder mystery with a seductively sexy love story featuring two of the decade's most attractive stars, the well-known James Stewart and the relative newcomer, Grace Kelly. The narrative plays with their screen personae: Stewart, Hollywood's most eligible bachelor until his recent marriage in 1949 at age 41, plays Jeff, a freedom-loving photographer who fears marriage because, as he tells his editor Gunnison, when he's married, he'll "never be able to go anywhere." Stewart's most famous postwar role – as George Bailey in Frank Capra's *It's a Wonderful Life* (1946) – explores this theme: George desperately wants to leave Bedford Falls, to become an engineer, and to build bridges in far-away countries, but is trapped in his hometown, initially by the needs of the family business and then by marriage and children.

Kelly had a somewhat notorious (off-screen) reputation for seducing her leading men.[6] For Hitchcock, Kelly was like "a snow covered volcano" – hot on the inside and icy cool on the outside.[7]

In *Rear Window,* he contrasts her overt sexual desire with her cool, quasi-aristocratic reserve. In the film, Kelly plays Lisa, a high-fashion career girl who will do almost anything, including moving "into an apartment across the way and do[ing] the dance of the seven veils every hour," to get the hero's attention.

The narrative is based, in large part, on a short story, "It Had to Be Murder," written by mystery/thriller novelist Cornell Woolrich in 1942. The original story, however, differs considerably from the script of the film. One chief difference is that Hitchcock and Hayes give the protagonist a profession – that of photojournalist – and a girlfriend. (Woolrich's hero's sole companion is a male, African-American "day houseman" named Sam, who takes care of him.) The reworking of the Woolrich story by Hitchcock and screenwriter John Michael Hayes also draws on aspects of biography, persona, and personal history. As Steve Cohen has pointed out, *Rear Window* is, in part, a reworking of the story of Ingrid Bergman and Robert Capa.[8]

Bergman met the famous war photographer, Robert Capa, in Paris in 1945 and immediately fell in love with him. When Bergman returned to Hollywood to star in Hitchcock's *Notorious* (1946), Capa accompanied her, taking photographs of her on the set for *Life* magazine. Hitchcock, according to biographer Donald Spoto, had become romantically obsessed with Bergman during the making of *Spellbound* (1945).[9] Hitchcock noted Bergman's passion for Capa as well as Capa's noncommittal responses to her. Bergman clearly wanted to marry the photographer, but he refused to, fearful of the commitment of marriage.[10] The Capa–Bergman affair dissolved within a year, largely over Capa's refusal to marry her. Cohen speculates that Hitchcock was amazed "that the photographer would walk away from a woman about whom he himself [Hitchcock] could only fantasize" and that the director deliberately set out to re-create this relationship several years later in *Rear Window*.

Cohen notes that the Jefferies character is subtly connected to Capa in the following ways: Both are photojournalists, both work for *Life* magazine,[11] both frequently eat at "21," and both live in Greenwich Village (within a block of one another).[12] Cohen concludes his comparison of Capa and Hitchcock's hero with the most bizarre and uncanny link between the two. "On May 25, 1954, two months before the release of *Rear Window*, Capa was taking photographs outside of Hanoi [in Vietnam] when he stepped on an anti-personnel mine. The explosion tore a gaping hole in his chest and blew off his left leg – the leg that Jefferies has in a cast. . . . By the time [Capa] was taken to a French field hospital, he was dead."[13] Production of the film had been completed by January (or at the latest, February) 1954, so Hitchcock could not possibly have known about Capa's left leg, but this final connection between life and art must certainly have astounded both Hitchcock and Bergman (if she ever realized that *Rear Window* was, in part, about her and Capa).

Aspects of star persona regularly play a role in the stories and themes of many motion pictures, but the role played by the biography of the director remains more problematic. Hitchcock never spoke of *Rear Window* in these terms (i.e., as "about" Bergman and Capa); nor was screenwriter John Michael Hayes aware of any connection between the scenario he wrote and the Bergman–Capa story; indeed, Hayes insists that the character of Lisa is based on his own wife, not Bergman.[14] But Hitchcock, who playfully acknowledges himself in the cameo appearances he makes in most of his films, was never one to refrain from including inside jokes or biographical allusions in his films. Indeed, *Rear Window* itself contains one such joke, played at the expense of Hitchcock's former producer, David O. Selznick, with whom the director repeatedly struggled for artistic control of his films. In directing Raymond Burr, who plays the villain Lars Thorwald, Hitchcock coached the actor to use various gestures and mannerisms that the director had seen his former employer use, especially the way Selznick cradled a telephone in the crook of his neck. Hitchcock also went out of his way to make Burr look like Selznick, giving him curly gray hair and making him wear the same style of glasses worn by the famous producer.

It would be foolish to place too much emphasis on the Bergman–Capa or the Selznick allusions; the film is not "about" them. The thematic concerns of the film cannot be reduced to biography. Nor should the critic engage in cheap psychoanalysis, proclaiming "eureka" when an aesthetic work can supposedly be traced back to some prior trauma or obsession of its creator. Ultimately, *Rear Window* is not about Bergman and Capa or about Hitchcock's obsession with Bergman. Nor, once its factual basis has been established, should such biographical detail be dismissed entirely. The film clearly is about the kind of relationship Bergman and Capa had – the aggressive pursuit by an attractive, glamorous, sexy, "perfect" woman of a man who fears commitment to her. But this theme remains one of many in a complex tapestry of related themes and ideas.

It's important to remember that the film is as much a product of classical Hollywood cinema as it is of Hitchcock or other creative personnel. The narrative deftly alternates back and forth between murder mystery and love story, intertwining the two through the theme of voyeurism. In this respect, the film is a perfect example of classical Hollywood cinema in that the narrative consists of "two plot lines: one involving heterosexual romance . . . , the other line involving another sphere – work, war, a mission or quest. . . . The story ends with . . . a resolution of the problem and a clear achievement or nonachievement of the [two] goals."[15] The hero's voyeurism links the two plot lines; it is clearly related to the murder mystery which he pieces together by looking out his window, but it is also connected to his relationship with the heroine. Refusing to commit himself to a love relationship, Jeff prefers looking out his window at his neighbors across the way to looking at Lisa, the beautiful blonde who is in the same room with him and who repeatedly throws herself at him. He opts for a one-way relationship based on voyeurism instead of a two-way relationship rooted in mutual regard, recognition, and concern; he would rather look than love.

The pleasure he derives from watching his neighbors without their knowledge or permission is essentially sadistic. (See Elise Lemire's discussion of feminist readings of the film in this volume.) It is a pleasure based on domination. A similar form of sadism emerges as a fundamental aspect of his relationship with the heroine. Lisa provides a willing exhibitionism in answer to his voyeurism: She wants to display herself to him. Thus, shortly after she first appears, she turns on lights one by one to introduce herself ("Lisa . . . Carol . . . Fremont") and to display her new $1,100 dress. But Jeff refuses her attempts to engage him in a mutual exchange of looking and being looked at. The film repeatedly opposes its two main "attractions" – Lisa and the murder mystery – and Jeff routinely turns his gaze from Lisa and focuses instead on events across the way.

Lisa's self-display is an attempt to control his gaze. Jeff, however, resists her strategy and tries, instead, to force Lisa to abandon her own attempts to control his gaze and to submit herself to *his* gaze, to join him in his voyeuristic activities. In other words, Jeff wants to enlist her in his own sadistic regime; he wants to dominate her. Though he himself, an invalid confined to a wheelchair, is weak, he attempts to achieve power over her by subjecting her not only to his "vision" – that is, his understanding of what is happening across the courtyard – but also to a form of emotional abuse. Jeff rejects Lisa's efforts to please him (the dinner from "21") and is deliberately rude to her after dinner, insisting that she "shut up" and let him talk. He toys with her, refusing to marry her, yet he remains unwilling to break off their affair.

The murder mystery initially provides the hero with an obsessive interest that he uses to avoid participation in the love story. Yet it also functions as a way of working out the tensions in that relationship. What Jeff represses in his relationship with Lisa is worked out in the actions seen across the way.[16] Thorwald's apparent murder of a nagging, invalid wife serves as a release of sorts for the hero from the threat posed by the heroine who has the immobilized hero at her mercy. The hero unconsciously identifies with the villain's desire to free himself from the responsibilities of his relationship with a woman who seeks to control him. Yet he would clearly never do what Thorwald apparently does: he consciously represses this desire and actively pursues the villain for his own would-be crime. The fact that the hero has so much trouble proving that the villain has killed his wife underscores the tenuous nature of his own identification with the forces of law and order. He remains torn between two desires – that of the villain and that of the villain's nemesis, the law. Jeff works out his feelings for Lisa by openly rejecting his identification with Thorwald, by relentlessly refusing to give up his belief in Thorwald's guilt. When he and Thorwald physically battle in the penultimate scene, he finally acts out – on a physical level – his opposition to the villain. Yet he also pays – with a second broken leg – for his (repressed) desire to do what Thorwald has done. Once Jeff's anxieties have been acted out, he can then resolve his relationship with Lisa. Though the film doesn't conclude with a marriage, it does present a final image of them as a more-or-less-stable couple.

If this is a very Freudian film, in which the villain functions as the Id to the hero's Super-ego, acting out his desires, it is also a very Catholic film. In projecting his desires, the hero becomes responsible for their acting-out by another. In the contemplation of evil, he becomes guilty of evil, even though he himself does not commit it. For Catholics like Hitchcock, the sin of omission – an immoral thought or desire that is repressed – is equal in the eyes of the Church to the sin of commission – an acting out of that illicit thought or desire. In this way, the double narrative remains tightly intertwined. *Rear Window,* as the title suggests, is a view onto unconscious desire: It looks into the back of the mind and at what it conceals. The eye is traditionally, for poets at least, a window into the soul; it is the "front" window, as it were. The unconscious mind, which opens onto a different terrain of desires, functions as a "rear" window: It sees what the eye does not. *Rear Window* explores the relationship between these two "windows," between what the eye sees and what the mind desires. What Jeff sees – the evidence of a murder – is what his mind unconsciously desires. The action of the film becomes a drama of catharsis – the purgation of his fears and desires by means of an acting out of them. His cure is achieved, quite appropriately, when Thorwald pushes him out of his rear window and, dragged down by the weight of his own body (and that of the heavy cast on his leg), he falls to the courtyard below.

Inasmuch as *Rear Window* is an "obvious" film, it wears all of these classical features, commercial "attractions," and manifest themes quite stylishly on its sleeve. But there is a great deal more to *Rear Window* than these obvious themes and commercial trappings. Admittedly, the film has its eye on the box office. It grossed $5.3 million in 1954, $4.5 million on its reissue in 1962, and another $12 million on its re-release in 1983, making it director Alfred Hitchcock's most commercially successful film. But if the film has one eye on the box office, or "front" window, it also has its other eye on another, less obvious, decidedly "rear" window. It has noncommercial interests, looking at issues that, most properly, belong to the domains of film theory, criticism, history, and aesthetics. Its story and the way that story is told raise questions about the nature of the cinema itself. In this respect, *Rear Window* is Hitchcock's "testament" film – that is, it is a film that is "about" the cinema, a film that serves as a director's ultimate statement about his or her craft.

In other words, what is least obvious about the film is its own artistry. Like most Hollywood films, *Rear Window* strives for transparency. Its story and its characters are delivered to the audience simply and directly, as if they were just "there." All signs that might reveal the artifice of the film's production or construction have been carefully effaced. Yet *Rear Window* (like Hitchcock films in general) is not entirely transparent. It is carefully constructed. As narrator, Hitchcock maintains a visible presence that goes far beyond his cameo appearance. *Rear Window* is, after all, a Hitchcock film, marked by his dark sensibility, by his wry wit, and by his intrusive presence as a storyteller.

Hitchcock's visibility as a narrator has become part of his "contractual" relationship with his audiences. Viewers expect a Hitchcock film to be "Hitchcockian" – that is, to have a certain kind of narrative sensibility – much as they expect Hitchcock's own cameo appearances within the films themselves. (In *Rear Window*, Hitch appears in the Song Writer's apartment [reel 2A, shot 44] winding a clock, just before Jeff and Lisa sit down to a lobster dinner from "21.")[17] By means of this sort of visibility, Hitchcock vio-

A Film about Looking: Voyeurism escalates and becomes contagious. Jeff (James Stewart) starts looking with his naked eye, then with binoculars, and finally with a telephoto lens. Here Stella (Thelma Ritter) joins in. Note the smashed camera on the table in the background – a symbol of prior punishment for voyeurism. Photo courtesy of Paramount.

lates the norms of classical Hollywood cinema; he winks, as it were, at the audience, and conspires with them in constructing the illusion of the fiction; he thus acknowledges that the film *is* a construction and that *he* has constructed it.[18]

A self-reflexive work, the film is about looking. Jeff serves as a surrogate for the spectator. Seated in his chair and unable to move, he looks, through a frame that resembles that of the screen, at events that take place in a semidistant space. His activity is like that of a typical spectator: He attempts to make sense out of – to read – what he sees. Thus he constructs a narrative out of the disparate actions that occur within his view. This is what all film spectators do.[19] Jeff, however, crosses the line; driven by his desire for more knowledge, he "invades" the space across the way, sending Lisa into it to deliver threatening messages to Thorwald. This violates the traditional "segregation of spaces" that defines cinematic spectatorship in which the space of the spectator remains distinct from that of the action on the screen. The penalty for this transgression is Lisa's terrorization by Thorwald, followed by Thorwald's entry into Jeff's space. In effect, Hitchcock explores the nightmarish consequences of voyeurism – what happens to a spectator when he or she looks and is unprotected by the conventions that safeguard the typical film spectator.

The fact that Jeff is a photographer – a professional voyeur – reinforces the notion that *Rear Window,* as a testament film, is about the consequences of looking. The accident that put Jeff in a cast is presumably a consequence of his professional desire to see; he got too close to the action he wanted to photograph and was hit by a race car. The film's backstory (the circumstances surrounding the accident) thus establishes a logic that connects looking to its consequences. Whatever pleasures derive from voyeurism are accompanied by anxiety and pain – by the fear of being seen and by punishment for having seen. Jeff sees Thorwald as the latter finally sees him. Now seen, Jeff suddenly becomes the victim of the villain's gaze. The disturbed nature of this transfer of vision from Jeff to Thorwald is conveyed in the penultimate scene in which we share Thorwald's point of view as he is blinded by the exploding flashbulbs of Jeff's camera. When we see from Thorwald's point of view, we suddenly experience Thorwald's pain and displeasure. The film takes us full circle from voyeuristic pleasure to voyeuristic pain. Yet it works out this shift in a way that reinstates and supports the spectator's right to look. (Jeff's voyeurism is vindicated in that it leads to the apprehension of a murderer; the villain's appropriation of that look is seen as a disturbance that is inappropriate and is thus presented as painful via red suffusions.)

Rear Window observes the principles that shape classical Hollywood narratives – economy, regularity, symmetry, and order. It is systematic; all of its elements are part of a larger formal system. The functions of its various elements are driven by the demands of the narrative. Every event serves a narrative purpose; in this way, the film observes the principle of economy. Events are presented in terms of their function within a larger narrative structure; one feature of this "economy" is that they are organized according to the principles of regularity, symmetry, and order. The film is constructed around instances of repetition and variation (of motifs and specific shots). These motifs and shots are organized into a larger pattern. This pattern underlies the film's construction.

As a construction, *Rear Window* is classically Aristotelian: It has a beginning, a middle, and an end; it observes the basic Aristotelian unities – unity of action, unity of place, and, given some ellipses, unity of time.[20] These points of time (the beginning, middle, and end) punctuate the narrative in a fairly obvious, theatrical way. Whatever abstract significance the title of the film may have, the rear window functions quite literally to mark the stages of the film's narrative progression. At the same time, it characterizes that narrative as theatrical spectacle. The film's credit sequence begins with the rear window and with the raising of its three bamboo curtains to reveal the courtyard beyond Jeff's window. The film ends with the lowering of these three curtains. (The mid-1980s re-release prints of the film, distributed by Universal, omit this last shot because it contains the logo of the film's original distributor, Paramount. This omission seriously distorts the formal design of the film. Universal's recent restoration of the film recognizes the significance of this earlier deletion and includes the final lowering of the curtains.)[21]

In the "middle" of the film (reel 5A, shots 43 and 47), Lisa lowers, then raises, the curtains. The initial opening of the curtains "opens" the narrative, presenting it as if it were a spectacle at the theater, where the raising and lowering of the curtain would punctuate breaks between acts. The final curtain "closes off" the narrative, signaling to audiences that all the various enigmas raised earlier in the narrative have been resolved. Both of these actions are performed by Hitchcock. They are nondiegetic events; the raising and lowering of the curtains is performed by an unseen agent (a presence connected with the presentation of the credits). In contrast, the lowering and raising of the curtains in reel 5 are diegetic events. This action is performed by a character within the film (Lisa).

Though it does not literally occur in the middle of the film, Lisa's action does break the narrative into two halves.[22] Lisa lowers the curtain in a false resolution of sorts. Lt. Doyle has just left after informing Jeff and Lisa that there has been no murder and that "there is no case to be through with." After watching Miss Lonely Hearts entertain then struggle with a would-be lover, Jeff and Lisa question the ethics of watching neighbors "with binoculars and a long-focus lens." Lisa then closes the blinds, providing herself as another spectacle to take the place of Jeff's previous interest in his neighbors. Declaring (in suitably appropriate, theatrical language) that the "show's over for tonight," she displays the nightgown that she has brought with her, describing it as a "preview of coming attractions." The case has been closed; the mystery is over and the love story has reached a climax of sorts. Fade out.

But wait. The film is not over. It fades back in. Lisa models her nightgown. A woman screams off-screen. Lisa raises the blinds to look and discovers a second murder, that of a dog who "knew too much." With the scream (which recalls the disembodied scream Jeff hears on the night of Mrs. Thorwald's murder) and the opening of the blinds, the murder-mystery narrative resumes. Jeff declares that Doyle was wrong: Thorwald did murder his wife and killed the dog because it was too curious about what Thorwald had buried in his flower bed. With the death of the dog, the film suddenly reverses itself. Prior to this moment, Jeff has been primarily a voyeur. After it, he becomes a *provocateur*. He continues to look, but he also takes action. In the first part of the film, the spaces have been separate – Jeff's apartment occupies one space and the apartments across the way occupy another. At the same time, the voyeurism has been unidirectional; Jeff and others look from his apartment at apartments across the way. In the second part, the segregation of spaces is constantly violated. Jeff immediately dispatches Lisa with a blackmail note ("What have you done with her?") which she delivers to Thorwald's apartment. A few moments later, Lisa invades the apartment in search of evidence.

This intrusion is answered by Thorwald, who catches Lisa, realizes that Jeff has been spying on him, and then attacks Jeff in his own apartment. Thorwald thus reverses the direction of the narrative. From looking at Thorwald, Jeff becomes looked at: Lisa's screams for Jeff direct Thorwald to him. Jeff's point of view, which has dominated the film so far, gives way momentarily to Thorwald's. We see through his eyes, via red suffusions, as Jeff attempts to blind Thorwald with flashbulbs. Jeff's point-of-view shots end at the moment that Thorwald begins to stalk him. Jeff's audio point of view is suddenly foregrounded and expressionistically heightened. He hears Thorwald's footsteps as he clumps up the stairs, walks down Jeff's hallway, and unscrews the hallway light. Thorwald, who had been a silent presence until now, speaks for the first time, asking "What do you want from me?"

The dog's death emerges as a pivotal moment in this dramatic shift in point of view. For the first time, the camera abandons the position it has occupied since the beginning of the film (its vantage point from Jeff's rear window) and situates itself within the courtyard area, looking up from the garden at the Siffleuse (literally "the whistler," better known in the film as the dog's mistress), Miss Torso, and others. Though the initial point of view from Jeff's apartment returns after this brief disruption, the grip it holds on the film has been undermined; its future stability can no longer be assured. Thus, a few minutes later Thorwald grapples with Jeff and pushes him out of his apartment through the rear window. At this point, the film cuts to a perspective that previously had been suppressed; we see Jeff hanging from his windowsill from the vantage point of Doyle and the neighbors across the way. For the first time, we see the rear wall of Jeff's apartment building and the rear window from its reverse side. This shift in point of view forces us to rethink Jeff's and our own role as spectators. For a moment, it is our own voyeurism that has become the film's spectacle. The tracking shot at the end of the opening credits that takes us through the rear window and displays for us the world of the film and draws us into it here has its answering look. From the other side of this world, we look back and see Jeff, our surrogate as spectator within the film, suddenly small and helpless in the frame. At risk for the first time in the film, he pays the price of his voyeurism with a fall out of his own rear window and with a second broken leg.

The final shots of the film recall the first shots. A single crane shot around the courtyard records the resolution of all the narratives introduced in the film's first few shots, which provided similar surveys of the courtyard. Miss Lonely Hearts and the Song Writer are now together; the Thorwalds' apartment is being repainted and readied for new occupants; the Siffleuse and her husband have a new dog; Miss Torso welcomes home her boyfriend, a dumpy-looking soldier; the Newlyweds squabble; and Lisa is now a permanent fixture in Jeff's apartment, supervising his recovery. With the resolution of the mystery, Jeff peacefully sleeps; this last image of him thus recalls the first image of him, asleep with his back to the rear window.

The formal structure of the film underscores its meaning. The opening and closing shots link a survey of the characters in the courtyard to the back of Jeff's head, which "faces" out the rear window. The implication is that what he sees through this window is an extension of his unconscious mind, of the back of his head. During the course of the film, Jeff repeatedly turns and looks out the window. Crane shots (culminating with shots of Jeff asleep) give way to point-of-view and reaction shots, as he watches his neighbors. Through the conscious activity of his gaze, he attempts to make sense out of unusual, enigmatic, puzzling, and irrational occurrences. He imposes logic and meaning on a human activity that ultimately defies understanding. What sense does it make for a man to kill his wife because she nags too much or for a lonely woman to try to kill herself? As Armond White suggests later in this volume, Jeff's vigilance keeps chaos at bay; his voyeurism is an attempt to defeat disturbances out there in the world of 1950s America. Or better yet, his conscious gaze functions to regulate and render harmless his (and our) unconscious desires. In other words, the film's structure announces and maps out the interconnection between the conscious and the unconscious mind, between active voyeurism and passive, vaguely articulated, unconscious desire. The film is *about* looking and desire; it is *about* the interaction of conscious and unconscious activity; it is *about* the processes and activities of the cinema as it engages its spectators in the attractions that define it as "entertainment," as a form of mass amusement that holds us in its thrall.

In the essays that follow, *Rear Window* is explored from a variety of vantage points, or "looks." Each chapter reconstructs the film from a distinct perspective; the anthology thus provides a vision of the film that expands upon the restricted vision that lies at the core of the film. These various perspectives will hopefully enable readers to see more clearly how the film actually works. Scott Curtis provides a detailed production history of the film, drawing on studio production files housed at the Academy of Motion Picture Arts and Sciences. At the same time, he links the production of the film to certain notions of construction within it, ranging from the literal construction of the sets and the physical filming process to the film's more abstract concern with the construction of meaning by the film's central character, Jeff, as well as by the film's spectator.

Elise Lemire discusses *Rear Window* in terms of feminist film theorist Laura Mulvey's use of the film as an example of the patriarchal nature of classical Hollywood cinema and the gendered nature of film spectatorship. Lemire contrasts Mulvey's reading of the film with theorist Tania Modleski's critique of Mulvey's reading in an attempt to understand exactly how the film addresses female spectators and how it both supports and subverts the paradigms of patriarchal cinema. Lemire complements the psychoanalytic readings of the film by Mulvey and Modleski with her own, "cultural studies" reading. Situating the film within various discourses on masculinity and female sexuality in postwar America, she argues that *Rear Window* explores male anxiety in the face of radical changes in the professional and sexual identity of women in 1950s America.

Sarah Street looks at *Rear Window* from the angle of fashion and costume design. For Street, Hitchcock maximizes the function of fashion by enlisting it to convey crucial plot points, gender distinctions, and class relations, as well as serving as a vehicle that could be manipulated by specific (female) characters for purposes of masquerade and transgressive control of their own image. In this way, the film can be read through its fashions, which comprise a discourse on the film's narrative mechanisms, character relationships, and themes.

Michel Chion discusses the construction of the film's space – both that of the courtyard and that of Jeff's apartment – in relation to its hero's point of view. At the same time, Chion explores the film's careful manipulation of the soundtrack to direct both the hero's and the spectator's attention through this space.

In his chapter, Armond White analyzes the film in terms of the social and political landscape of 1950s American culture. Until recently, Hitchcock's work has been viewed as apolitical.[23] White calls attention to the film's representation of the social (the courtyard, the alienated figures gathered together around it) and to the political implications of these images. This study provides a foundation for White to explore subsequent reworkings of elements of the film's theme, plot, and character by other, more overtly "political" directors. In particular, he deals with Michelangelo Antonioni's *Blow-Up* (1966), Francis Ford Coppola's *The Conversation* (1974), and Brian De Palma's *Sisters* (1973) and *Blow Out* (1981).

The anthology also includes contemporary reviews of the film (including a review by composer Stephen Sondheim) published shortly after its release in 1954.

NOTES

1. *The Film Daily Year Book* voted it one of the ten best pictures of 1954, ranking it third behind *The Caine Mutiny* and *On the Waterfront. The 1956 Film Daily Year Book of Motion Pictures,* ed. Jack Alicoate (New York: The Film Daily, 1956), 125.
2. Paramount's "Detail Production Cost" memo, dated December 31, 1955 and reproduced at the end of Chapter 1, indicates that the film was shot in widescreen and in stereo sound. Though not filmed in VistaVision (Paramount's proprietary large-format, widescreen system), it was designed to be masked in projection to conform with the studio's preferred 1.66:1 aspect ratio (ratio of width to height). It is not clear that all theaters projected the film in widescreen on its release, and there is no additional evidence that it was recorded in stereo sound. At this point in its history, Paramount was using a pseudostereo, optical sound system known as Perspecta Sound. This system enabled films recorded monaurally to be played back in the theater in stereo.

3. See Tom Gunning, "The Cinema of Attractions: Early Film, Its Spectator, and the Avant-Garde," *Wide Angle* 8, Nos. 3/4 (Fall 1986), 63–70.
4. The quoted text comes from the front page of Paramount's original 1954 "Showmanship Manual" (press book) for the film. This ad also features many of the windows across the way, accompanied by captions highlighting the sensational aspects of the characters associated with these windows. Thus "MISS TORSO – Hot nights or cold, her shades were never drawn!"
5. Joe Hyams, "Hitchcock's *Rear Window*," *New York Herald Tribune,* August 1, 1954.
6. Kelly reportedly seduced the married Ray Milland, her co-star in Hitchcock's *Dial M for Murder,* 1954, and, at the time, Hitchcock commented on her promiscuity to an interviewer. See Robert Lacey, *Grace* (New York: G. P. Putnam's Sons, 1994), 138, 140.
7. Lacey, 11.
8. Steve Cohen, "*Rear Window:* The Untold Story," *Columbia Film View* 8, No. 1 (Winter/Spring 1990): 2–7. I want to thank Scott Curtis for bringing this essay to my attention.
9. Donald Spoto, *The Dark Side of Genius: The Life of Alfred Hitchcock* (Boston: Little, Brown, 1983), 307–308.
10. Capa's relationships with women and his fear of commitment are discussed by his biographer, Richard Whelan, in *Robert Capa: A Biography* (New York: Knopf, 1985), passim.
11. *Life* refused to give Hitchcock permission to use its name in the film, but the design of the cover of the magazine on which Jeff's fashion photo appears (it is a positive print of the negative seen framed in Jeff's apartment) is clearly modeled on that of *Life.*
12. Capa lived on 9th St.; Jefferies lives within view of Thorwald's apartment, which Lisa tells us is at 125 West 9th St. See Cohen, 5. There is a reference to "21" in Hitchcock's first film with Bergman, *Spellbound.* Playing a psychoanalyst, Bergman interprets the hero's dream about cards, the suit of clubs and 21, as a reference to the 21 Club in New York.
13. Cohen, 6–7.
14. In an interview with Steve Cohen, Hayes denied any knowledge of the story's indebtedness to the Bergman–Capa affair. Indeed, he insisted that the Kelly character, Lisa, was modeled on his own wife, not on Bergman. Cohen, 6.
15. Bordwell, "Classical Hollywood Cinema: Narrative Principles and Procedures," in *Narrative, Apparatus, Ideology,* ed. Philip Rosen. New York: Columbia University Press, 1985, 18, 19.
16. See Robin Wood's "Rear Window" in his *Hitchcock's Films Revisited* (New York: Columbia University Press, 1989), 102.
17. Reel and shot references are based on *Rear Window: Release Dialogue Script, June 21, 1954* (in the author's collection).
18. An acquaintance of mine once suggested that the rear window of

Jeff's apartment was like the lens of a camera and the apartment itself was like the interior of a camera. When Thorwald enters, he opens "the camera" and exposes "the negative film." Since Jeff never takes a picture during the course of the film, this analogy might have some credibility in that the notion of the camera functions largely on a metaphorical rather than literal level.

19. In *Narration in the Fiction Film*, David Bordwell discusses Jeff's role in terms of the activities of the typical spectator, who constructs a story out of plot events. See *Narration in the Fiction Film* (Madison: University of Wisconsin Press, 1985), 40–47.

20. The film appears to cover four consecutive days as well as an unspecified fifth day. It progresses from a "run-of-the-mill Wednesday" to a climactic Saturday (when Thorwald throws Jeff out the window), followed by an unspecified later date (when Jeff has been treated and released from the hospital, the Song Writer's composition has been recorded, and time enough has elapsed for Thorwald's landlord to begin the repainting of his apartment).

21. The "text" of *Rear Window* was significantly altered once again during the mid-1980s for a television broadcast version of the film. In 1986, in order to fit the film into a two and one-half hour time slot, MCA-TV prepared a "long" version of the film by reformatting the original, which ran at 24 frames per second, to run at 23 frames per second and by adding dream sequences. On the night that Thorwald goes out again and again in the rain carrying his sample case, Jeff sleeps fitfully. During one of his slumbers, MCA inserted "a three-minute montage of footage and nonsynchronous dialogue from earlier in the film." This version was apparently withdrawn from circulation shortly after it was aired in February or March of 1986. For a discussion of this version, see Joseph L. Streich, "Reinventing the Wheel: How TV Remakes the Classics," *The Village Voice* (March 11, 1986).

22. Lisa lowers the curtain near the end of the film in Reel 5A, shot 43; she raises it moments later, in the same reel, during shot 47. The film has six 2,000-foot reels.

23. For a sociopolitical reading of Hitchcock, see Robert Corber's *In the Name of National Security: Hitchcock, Homophobia, and the Political Construction of Gender in Postwar America* (Durham, NC: Duke University Press, 1993).

1 The Making of *Rear Window*

In the contemporary advertisements for *Rear Window,* the set looms large above the actors as the most prominent feature. In the publicity releases Paramount sent to the press, a description and history of the set is featured second only to a blurb about Hitchcock. In the black-and-white trailers made especially for television, there are no actors at all, only a slow pan around the courtyard set, accompanied by voice-over narration. In many ways, then, the fabulous set built for *Rear Window* is the "star" of the film, even more central to its success than James Stewart or Grace Kelly. It certainly cost more than the actors: Designing, constructing, dressing, and lighting the set accounted for over 25 percent of the total cost of the picture, compared to 12 percent for the cast.[1] Robert Burks, *Rear Window*'s director of photography, did not exaggerate when he called the undertaking the biggest production on a Paramount lot since the days of Cecil B. DeMille.[2]

Given the significance of the set for the film, it is only fitting that this chapter reflect that importance by providing an "architectural" history of the project. The following, therefore, is something of a backstage tour of the production, an inspection of the nuts and bolts, the girders and planks with which *Rear Window* was "built." This chapter describes the evolution of the production from the ground up: the acquisition of the property that provided its foundation, the design of the film, the construction of the set, the principal photography, the final touches, and the window dressing. By retracing the construction of *Rear Window,* we can create a "blueprint" of the film that will provide insight into the structure of this and other Hitchcock productions as well as the principles behind the production of Hollywood studio films in general.

It would be wholly appropriate, too, if this "blueprint" somehow mirrored the film's themes and design; it has become a critical commonplace that *Rear Window* is among the most reflexive of all films.[3] If, as John Belton maintains, "the film is engaged in a playful acknowledgment of its own constructedness," then we can examine the film *and* its production history as an allegory of the construction of meaning.[4] From the original story that provides the "plot" upon which the film is built, to the narratively meaningful set design and photography, to the subsequent publicity campaign's slight "remodeling" of the story, each stage of the film's construction echoes the interpretive work of both Jefferies and the spectator.

THE PROPERTY

How did Hitchcock come across this "property," this "plot" upon which he could "build to suit"? That is, how did he come to make a film of Cornell Woolrich's short story, "Rear Window"? One might guess that he read the story, liked it, and decided to buy it. Actually – and this is more indicative of the way deals are usually made in Hollywood – a string of agents and executives led him to material that fit his needs at the time. The paper trail begins in February 1942, when *Dime Detective Magazine* published a short story by Woolrich, writing as William Irish, titled "It Had to Be Murder."[5] In 1944 Woolrich gathered this story – renaming it "Rear Window" – and five others in an anthology titled *After-Dinner Story*. The publisher, J. B. Lippincott, submitted the anthology to Paramount Pictures (and to many other studios, we can be sure) that same year and a studio reader dutifully provided a summary of the story's salient features and general adaptability, which was subsequently filed for posterity.[6]

H. N. Swanson, Woolrich's literary agent, sold the film rights to the stories in *After-Dinner Story* to B. G. De Sylva Productions for $9,250 in 1945.[7] Buddy De Sylva, a well-known stage and film producer, made his fortune by buying and selling rights to musical and literary properties. When he died in 1950, his rights to the anthology went up for auction and Leland Hayward, a stage producer and talent agent, along with Joshua Logan, a Broadway playwright and director, bought them up for a pittance.[8] Logan wrote a treatment of "Rear Window" in February 1952.[9] According to Logan, he and Hayward planned to produce "Rear Window" as a "trial balloon" in order to test studio and audience reaction to his film-directing skills before attempting to direct his Broadway hit, *Mister Roberts,* for the big screen. (Up to that point, Logan had little feature filmmaking experience.)[10] But this plan was eventually scuttled; in April 1953 Hayward sent Logan's treatment to Lew Wasserman, Hitchcock's agent at MCA in New York.[11]

At this time, Hitchcock was preparing his latest film for Warner Bros., *Dial M for Murder,* while Wasserman negotiated for him a multipicture contract with Paramount.[12] Wasserman forwarded the treatment to Hitchcock, undoubtedly thinking that it would make suitable material for the first of these pictures. James Stewart was a part of the plan from the beginning; following *Rope* (1948), he and Hitchcock planned to make another film together and as early as May 1953 they are named, along with Hayward and Logan, as producers of this new film.[13] The situation was very cozy: Not only were Stewart and Logan old friends and classmates at Princeton (and members of Princeton's University Players in the early 1930s), but Hitchcock, Stewart, and Logan all shared the same agent – Lew Wasserman.[14]

This might also explain the sweet deal Hayward and Logan received for their efforts: Some time between May and November 1953, Patron, Inc., the production company formed by Hitchcock and Stewart, bought the story rights from Hayward and Logan for $10,000. In addition, Logan received a tidy $15,000 for his thirteen-page treatment.[15] The deal may have been even sweeter. According to the budget sheets, the $10,000 covered only a *portion* of the story rights; the balance was to be paid from the film's revenues. An outline titled "Legal Notes Relative to Haygan [*Hay*ward-*Logan*] Incorporated – 'Rear Window,'" states, "The services of the producer, director, James Stewart, including the services of Haygan's attorney, will not exceed $200,000; all of which will be deferred and payable out of the gross receipts of the photoplay. . . . Allow $10,000 in budget for Story Rights. Balance of Story Rights are to be recouped from $200,000 deferred charge."[16] In other words, Hitchcock, Stewart, and Haygan were paid out of this $200,000 slice of the revenues. The outline also implies that Haygan is the production company, but Patron, Inc. is listed as the production company on the Paramount budgets, the earliest of which is dated October 8, 1953. So while Hayward and Logan were not the final producers of record, they might have received further considerations after the film's release.[17] Stewart and Hitchcock remained sole owners of the film; they received an *initial* payment for their services from the $200,000 mentioned here, but retained rights to the film's *future* profits, after Paramount's eight-year license. Stewart, by the way, was one of the first actors in Hollywood to defer his salary for a percentage of the film's profits, a practice that is commonplace today.

Hitchcock had his contract with Paramount by June 1953 and clearly planned to make *Rear Window* as his first Paramount film. During the next few months, however, he was busy with *Dial M for Murder,* which was to be shot in the new 3-D process; principal photography began August 5 and ended September 25.[18] Hitchcock did some preproduction planning for *Rear Window* while shooting *Dial M,* but it was only toward the end of September that he could devote all his time to the Paramount project. Grace Kelly, the star of *Dial M,* remembered that, during the frustrations of filming in 3-D, "the only reason he could remain calm was because he was already preparing for his next picture, *Rear Window.* He sat and talked to me about it all the time, even before we had discussed my being in it. He was very enthusiastic as he described all the details of a fabulous set while we were waiting for the camera to be pushed around."[19]

The screenwriter, John Michael Hayes, also came to the project via Hitchcock's agents. Hayes recalls, "We had the same agents at MCA, and they thought that my radio background in comedy and suspense might make me acceptable to him. He already owned the Woolrich short story and they suggested I work with him on it."[20] Hayes also explains, "I first met Alfred Hitchcock on the set of *Dial M for Murder*. We had a story conference in which we discussed generally the outline we were going to use and what we had to add to it."[21] While Logan might have broken ground first on Woolrich's property, the construction began in earnest as Hayes finished a seventy-six-page treatment of the story in early September 1953.[22] With this in hand, Paramount could budget the film and Hitchcock could begin its design once principal photography for *Dial M* was complete.

PREPRODUCTION

If writing the treatment can be likened to clearing and surveying the "plot," a film's unique design begins to take shape only with the storyboard, art direction, and final script. Once the property is secured, however, budgeting is the next step in the process. As a rule, accountants at the studios divide any given film's costs into approximately thirty general categories, which correspond to the studio's various departments (wardrobe, set construction, etc.). (See examples at the end of this chapter.) These categories are arranged on the budget sheet according to their place in a production's evolution, from story to sound recording. Costs are estimated based upon a treatment or, preferably, a finished screenplay. The story department makes multiple copies of the property and sends them to the departments, each of which returns its cost estimate of the work necessary to produce it. If the first budget is based upon a treatment, then the process begins again when the finished screenplay arrives.

In this particular case, budgeting began as soon as MCA sent Hayes's treatment to Paramount on September 11.[23] The Paramount accountants prepared a preliminary budget by October 8, but as Hayes turned in completed pages of the screenplay, the

budgeting continued through principal photography, ending with
the November 30 budget. The difference between the estimates
could be considerable. For example, the "Lighting" estimate bal-
looned from $15,726 on the October 8 budget to $65,000 on the
November 30 tally. The decision to "prelight" each apartment on
the set contributed to this huge increase. The total budget went
from $598,000 at the beginning of October to $875,000 at the
start of shooting. However, the principal players (other than Stewart) had not signed as of October 8, so their cost alone contributed
over $93,000 of that budget increase; clearly, these additions were
expected and not unusual.[24]

As the budgeting process rolled along, Hitchcock began work
on the visual design of the film, creating a cinematic story out of
the plot Hayes's treatment provided. Hayes recalls:

> When he finished *Dial M for Murder* we went to his office at Para-
> mount and sat down with the script. We went over it line by line
> and page by page. What we did then was try to break it up into
> shots. Now Hitch wanted to set them up into actual camera
> angles. He had a large sketch pad on which he sketched out each
> camera set-up for each scene. . . . He didn't wait until he got onto
> the set. He had the whole thing done when we finished working
> on the script in his office. He put the sketches in a large book. The
> camera men and the assistant directors looked at the sketches and
> Hitch told them what he wanted done.[25]

The use of a storyboard was typical of Hitchcock's working
method, but not typical of Hollywood studio practice. While more
meticulous directors – notably Orson Welles and Fred Zinnemann
– would often sketch out certain scenes in their films, the use of a
storyboard for an entire film was relatively rare in Hollywood film
making outside of animated features and special cases such as
Gone with the Wind.[26] Hitchcock's experience as an art director in
the 1920s undoubtedly contributed to his habit of sketching out
the shots of all his films beforehand. (Skilled draftsman though he
was, he usually had a graphic artist turn his sketches into more
substantial storyboard images.) He often said that his delight in
film making came from inventing the visual aspects of a film: "I

wish I didn't have to shoot the picture. When I've gone through the script and created the picture on paper, for me the creative job is done and the rest is just a bore."[27]

With a preliminary storyboard in place, hung on the walls of his office, important members of his crew discussed the production design in greater detail. John Woodcock, the assistant editor assigned to the film, remembers these meetings:

> My introduction to our famous producer/director came at a preproduction meeting in his office, which was also attended by Bob Burks (director of photography), Lenny South (camera operator) and a man who turned out to be a graphic artist. . . . [M]y immediate attention was attracted to what seemed like cartoon panels covering three walls of the large room. It turned out to be a storyboard – the first that I had ever seen – in which every scene in the picture was portrayed by simple sketches that indicated the camera angle and action. . . . It was kept up to date and changed to reflect any changes in the actual shooting and was used to great effect in *Rear Window*.[28]

That even the editors were at the meeting illustrates the importance of the storyboards for the entire production. Editors for most studio productions were not usually involved until the postproduction phase, after principal photography was complete. Hitchcock brought George Tomasini, the supervising editor, and Woodcock along because they were expected to cut the film as the storyboard dictated. "Thank God for the storyboard," Woodcock says, "we even had a copy to assist in the editing."[29] The film therefore came to the editors "precut": The order of the shots had already been determined even before shooting began. The storyboard, then, not only was one of the first stages in the construction of meaning – in the sense that camera angles and editing choices were first given their narrative significance here – but also served as the primary means by which Hitchcock articulated and maintained his authorial voice.

Hitchcock had a hand in the art direction, too. Although Hal Periera, the head of Paramount's art department, acted in a general supervisory capacity and received top credit, Joseph MacMillan

"Mac" Johnson actually designed the set and supervised its construction. While Hayes retreated to finish the screenplay, Hitchcock, Johnson, and Periera began to sketch the set from the storyboards. It was clear from the beginning that the nature of the film required a studio set, rather than location shooting; to take over an actual apartment complex for two months and attempt to control the elements was simply out of the question. Besides, the confinement of *Rear Window* to a single studio set mirrored Jeff's own confinement to his apartment and offered Hitchcock the sort of challenge he clearly enjoyed. (Compare, for example, similar restrictions in *Lifeboat, Dial M,* or *Rope.*) It also presented a challenge to the production designers: how to express the themes of the entire film through a single set?

John Belton argues that Jeff's immobility determines the structure of the set and narrative. For example, the decision to limit the action to a single setting meant that narrative tangents, or subplots, had to be limited to this setting as well and therefore built into the stage design. The film does not cut away to events across town because all of the necessary elements have been built into the set. Jeff need look no further than his own backyard for a story. Furthermore, the film's central theme of spectatorship is expressed through this design: The set has been built from Jeff's point of view, or as Belton puts it, "The set has been built for the camera and for the cinema spectator, placing them at its central station point." That Jeff's apartment acted as the center of operations during principal photography – all lighting, sound, and camera work was controlled from this point, as we shall see – only reinforces the idea that "the set design reproduces the conditions of spectatorship in the conventional movie theater." Immobile and voyeuristic, Jeff is watching several different movies at once – the designers even matched the size of the windows to different screen aspect ratios.[30]

If his neighbors are somehow unified by Jeff's point of view, they are still physically and emotionally isolated from him and each other. Even though they share a common space – the courtyard – it is just as fragmented and inviolate as the apartments; its

The Courtyard Set: Prominent in advertising copy, the colossal set was the most elaborate bit of art design at Paramount since the days of Cecil B. DeMille. Photo courtesy of Paramount.

maze of different levels and fences discourages anyone from entering another's area. (Contrast this situation to that in a Jean Renoir film, such as *The Crime of Monsieur Lange,* in which the courtyard is an emblem of community.) Likewise, Thorwald's apartment, with its wall separating the salesman from his wife, emphasizes the couple's estrangement. The set design, then, expresses the theme of isolation and alienation that runs throughout the film.

While designing the set to fit narrative demands, Hitchcock and Johnson were also concerned with realism. Toward the end of September, they sent C. O. "Doc" Erickson, the unit production manager for the film, to New York to obtain photographs of typical Greenwich Village courtyards. After making some preliminary sketches early in the process, Johnson sent photos of the drawings to Erickson with explicit instructions: "Find a rear court of this type of vista (sky and buildings in the background). This vista has to be north. . . . Take courtyard and vista in all its moods, dawn, morning, noon, afternoon, last rays of sunlight on B. G. [back-ground] buildings, dusk and night. . . . Shoot at least three differ-ent courts. Also shoot random color shots rear courtyards in the Village, for detail of color of buildings, any time of day. I will use these in painting the set."[31] These photographs helped Johnson pin down the details for his final sketches and helped Burks plan the huge task of lighting the entire set.

Construction of the set began on October 12 and was substan-tially complete by the time they started camera tests on November 13.[32] Built on Paramount's Stage 18, "the colossal set was 98 feet wide, 185 feet long, and 40 feet high, with structures rising five and six stories. . . . There were 31 apartments with most of the action occurring in eight completely furnished rooms, besides a labyrinth of fire escapes, roof-gardens, an alley, a street, and a sky-line."[33] The production notes from the studio publicity depart-ment claim that all the apartments in the building directly across from Jeff's had running water, electricity, and proper supporting from steel girders, so that they were actually habitable, though this might be a bit of hyperbole. They also claimed that "for the courtyard, laborers dug 30 feet below the stage level; so far, in fact, they struck water. This was determined when Harry Lindgren, the sound mixer, reported a strange noise creeping into the dialogue. When it was traced to running water, a small electric motor had to be installed to pump out the sump between camera takes."[34] The construction cost alone amounted to $72,505, with designing, dressing, operation and maintenance, and other related costs bringing the total to $192,087, which made it the single most expensive aspect of the entire production.[35] (See the list of produc-tion costs at the end of this chapter.)

Lighting the set turned into a daunting and expensive task. Paramount publicity trumpeted, "More than 1,000 giant arc-lights were needed to light the set from overhead, while more than 2,000 smaller variety of lamps were necessary for supplemental lighting."[36] Their figures might not be exact, but they do give a sense of the scale of the project. Burks himself declared, "Actually, lighting this composite set was the biggest electrical job ever undertaken on the lot by Paramount – not excepting even Cecil B. DeMille's big spectacle sets. Biggest, that is, in terms of number of electrical units used, amps used, and the number of individual light units and amount of cable laid. At one time, we had every switch on the lot in use on the sound stage."[37] The total cost of the lighting, including rentals, rigging, and operation (which would include the electric bill), came to $95,584.

Even so, it was less expensive than it might have been. Normally, electrical crews set up and strike lighting schemes for each shot, but given the size of the set and the several different points of action in any given shot of the courtyard, this procedure would have added days and dollars to the shooting schedule. Burks decided to "prelight" the set: "I went on the sound stage about ten days prior to the starting date. Using a skeleton crew, we pre-lit every one of the 31 apartments for both day and night, as well as lit the exterior of the courtyard for the dual-type illumination required. A remote switch controlled the lights in each apartment. On the stage, we had a switching set-up that looked like the console of the biggest organ ever made!"[38] As they were rigging the lights, Burks and his crew created a chart detailing the lighting plan for each room and indicating the switches to be thrown for any given lighting arrangement. So for a shot that included, for example, both Miss Lonely Hearts and Thorwald's apartments, Burks merely looked at his chart and flipped a few switches to turn on the necessary lights. While the lighting arrangements did require adjustments during principal photography, prelighting saved an enormous amount of time in the long run. A change in the set lighting from night to day required only 45 minutes or so.[39]

While Johnson and Burks constructed and lit the set, Hitchcock and Paramount worked to gather a cast. Stewart, of course, was on board from the beginning. Grace Kelly, with whom Hitchcock had first worked during *Dial M*, had always been his first choice for Lisa. Wendell Corey already had a contract with Paramount and fit nicely into the role of Detective Thomas J. Doyle. Hitchcock acquired Thelma Ritter from 20th Century-Fox, and even though she received fourth billing, she was the highest paid cast member,

garnering $25,694 for her work.[40] Raymond Burr, who at this point
in his career made a good living playing heavies (and, as John Belton notes, bears a remarkable resemblance in this film to another
Hitchcock bad guy, producer David O. Selznick), brought home
$8,541.[41] By prior agreement, Paramount paid the salaries of the
bit players and extras only; Patron, Inc. picked up the tab for the
speaking parts.

Meanwhile, Hayes was busy completing sections of the script.
He began turning in pages on October 20 and delivered steadily
until he finished at the end of November. Even though principal
photography began on November 27 without a completed screenplay, Hayes delivered a final draft within a few days of the start
date.[42] Studio policy required that the Breen Office of the Motion
Picture Association of America, which enforced the studio-spon-
sored Production Code, approve the script before shooting began.
Paramount sent the incomplete version of the October 20 script to
Joseph Breen; his office responded by November 20, objecting
mostly to the sexual suggestiveness and voyeuristic quality of the
screenplay. Concerning Miss Torso, for example, Breen wrote,
"The picturization of a young girl, described as wearing only black
panties, is unacceptable. It is apparent that she is nude above the
waist, and it is only by the most judicious selection of camera
angles that her nudity is concealed from the audience. We feel
that this gives the entire action a flavor of a peep show, which is
unacceptable."[43] Of course, this was the exact flavor Hitchcock
hoped to provoke and so he ignored most of their objections. But
it was eventually the set design itself – not any changes in the
script – that saved the film from the wrath of the Breen office.

PRINCIPAL PHOTOGRAPHY

The production opened on November 27 with a visit from
a delegation from the Breen office. In response to Breen's objections
to the script, Luigi Luraschi, the Paramount liaison to the MPAA,
suggested that the Production Code staff meet with Hitchcock on
the set. Luraschi and Hitchcock therefore anticipated Jeff's invita-

tion to Detective Doyle: "It's just something I can't tell you over the telephone. You have to be here and see the whole setup." The set design was so crucial to understanding the narrative that the Breen Office, like Doyle, had to make a special trip from "downtown." Such trips were rare and initiated always by the studio, never by the Office itself, which normally based its judgments on the script alone. But according to the memo from the delegation:

> [Luraschi] felt that some of the apprehension we had concerning stage directions would be eliminated, were we to see the physical set-up under which this action would be photographed. We readily agreed that the camera location, and the nature of this rather extraordinary set, eliminated much of the concern we felt in reading the script material. It is to be noted that the entire action will be photographed from a viewpoint of a man sitting in a wheelchair, looking out the window of his apartment. Many of the incidents which he observes, while described in great detail in the script, will be minimized by distance and camera angle in the shooting of this picture.[44]

This change of heart is remarkable because it provides evidence that the Breen Office sometimes considered film language – in this case, long shots and close-ups – when making their decision, rather than relying completely on the written word.[45] The reversal also mirrors or anticipates the reversal that each character experiences as he or she becomes convinced of Jeff's point of view. It seems that whoever occupies Jeff's (Hitchcock's) space slowly begins to see the events from his perspective. Ultimately, however, the Breen episode is somewhat ironic because the very distance that tempered their objections contributes to, even makes possible, the "peep show" quality that they condemned in the first place.

Though it solved political problems such as these, the size of the set also presented some technical difficulties. As noted earlier, the lighting schemes were controlled by a large console of remote-control switches, located in Jeff's apartment. The movements of the actors in the other apartments were guided in much the same way – not with switches, but with short-wave radio and hidden microphones. Every actor was fitted with a hidden microphone and flesh-colored headset, so that when cameras rolled from the vantage point of Jeff's apartment, Hitchcock could speak into the short-wave radio and direct the actors' pantomime by giving cues as they performed, much like silent film direction.[46]

The actors had to hit their marks exactly because the camera's long lenses had such a shallow depth of field; focus would be lost if an actor's movement varied a few inches either way. The camera crew normally determines the proper focusing distance by running a tape measure from the focal point of the camera to the action, but the distances across the courtyard obviously made this impractical for every setup. So during the prelighting operation, Burks and his assistants "premeasured" as well; they measured from the camera to points of action all around the courtyard, creating a comprehensive chart as they measured. So for any given shot, a glance at the chart provided the exact focusing distance.[47]

The power of the technician's glance to unify information and instigate action takes on special significance in this production. Many critics have argued that *Rear Window*'s core theme concerns the power of the (male) gaze.[48] From his unique position, seeing but not seen, Jeff controls the actions of others, such as when he persuades Doyle to investigate or calls Thorwald on the telephone or sends him cryptic notes.[49] Similarly, Hitchcock (with his short-wave radio) and his technicians (with their charts and consoles) see and manipulate the action from a privileged vantage point. Jeff's apartment becomes, in a way, the architectural embodiment of the themes of this film.

But if the film is a comment on film spectatorship, it is also a reflection on the craft of film making. From what he sees, Jeff pieces together a story from fragments of plot and, like a director, persuades others to act upon it. Just as Hitchcock built a story from the plot elements at hand, so Jeff (and the film spectator) fabricates a persuasive narrative from the snippets of evidence he sees. The construction of meaning always takes place at two points – during the writing and during the reading – but here we have a text that echoes *both* types of work. Alternately active and passive, Jeff embodies the activity and passivity of both the film

Behind the Scenes: Hitchcock (left) controlled the action across the courtyard by means of a short-wave radio installed in Jeff's apartment. The actors across the way wore flesh-colored earphones with frequencies tuned in to the shortwave signal. Here Hitchcock holds the short-wave microphone in his hand. Photo courtesy of the Academy of Motion Picture Arts and Sciences.

maker and the spectator; the director creates and waits, while the viewer sits and deliberates. Furthermore, Hitchcock's storyboard, Hayes's script, and Burks's charts are particularly graphic illustrations of this construction work and this reflexive theme.

Ironically, given the significance of the gaze for this film, focus and definition presented the main problems during the shooting. At first, Burks used a ten-inch lens for shots mimicking Jeff's view from behind his telephoto lens. But the depth of field was too shallow and objects did not show up clearly enough. For example, Jeff is looking through his long camera lens when Thorwald retrieves his wife's wedding ring. The point-of-view shot was filmed from across the courtyard through the ten-inch lens, but it wasn't clear that the object was a wedding ring. They tried it again with brighter lights so that they could stop down (that is, make the lens aperture smaller) and gain greater depth of field. It still didn't work, so they abandoned the lens, replaced it with a six-inch model, and compensated for the loss of magnification by placing the camera on a boom outside Jeff's apartment. Burks announced, "The results were sharp as a tack."[50]

All these lights generated a lot of heat, which of course could be very uncomfortable for the actors. It was no coincidence that the story takes place during a heat wave. The courtyard lighting for daylight was especially intense because there needed to be a balance between the light intensity inside the apartments (which, as small enclosed areas, required less light) and the intensity of the courtyard (which, as a large area, required more light). So to prevent actors from burning up as they approached the courtyard windows of their apartment, Burks installed graduated scrims (translucent cotton fabric stretched in a frame) to diffuse the courtyard lighting.[51] Even if the actors could stand the heat, sometimes the equipment could not. Stewart remembers:

> The lighting for some shots really created a problem. One day there were several shots where the camera was behind me – that is to say, I was in the foreground and across the courtyard the action was in focus. Well, you've got a big depth-of-field problem with that. It would need twice the amount of light, so that the aperture could be kept small to keep everything in focus. Paramount took all the lights they had from all the stages not in use and it still wasn't enough, then they borrowed lights from Columbia and MGM, and finally they could do the shot; the heat was really intense. Suddenly, in the middle of it, the lights set off the sprinkler system, not just a section of it, but on all the stages, and we're not talking about little streams of water but torrents. Everybody stopped as we were plunged into wet darkness. But it never fazed Hitchcock. He sat there and told his assistant to get the sprinklers shut off and then to tell him when the rain was going to stop, but in the meantime to bring him an umbrella.[52]

Fortunately, the set had been designed to deal, at least partially, with such problems. A complete drainage system had been installed to prevent flooding during the night scenes in which it rains; special "rain birds" – basically, glorified sprinklers – above the set provided this effect.[53]

The shots in which the courtyard is reflected in Jeff's telephoto lens also count as special effects. Because the successful filming of this reflection required precise control of its intensity relative to the ambient light, an image of the actual courtyard could not be captured. To solve this problem, the camera crew shot a transparency of the courtyard and projected the image onto a screen in front of Stewart, just out of camera range, so that the image would reflect off his lens.[54] Likewise, Jeff's climatic fall from his apartment window also required photographic effects. John P. Fulton, Paramount's special effects expert, used the "traveling matte" technique for this scene. Fulton first photographed the patio, shooting straight down from Jeff's window, with the detective and policeman poised to catch Stewart as he fell. Black velvet covered the area that Stewart would have occupied, effectively creating a "black hole" in the film. As the camera rolled, they acted as if they had just caught him. Then, several days later, in Paramount's Stage 3, they shot Stewart as he hung from a windowsill above mattresses covered with black velvet; he improvised his fall as the camera rolled. They could then superimpose this image onto the first and give the illusion that Jeff was falling out the window.[55] A body double and a dummy substituted for Stewart at other crucial points in the scene.[56]

Generally, the filming moved along smoothly, covering between four and seven pages of script a day. The daily production reports provide a precise summary of each day's shooting and the progress up to that point, which the studios typically measured in terms of pages per day. (See the example at the end of this chapter.) Having determined the principal photography start and finish dates well in advance of shooting, studio executives merely divided the number of pages by the number of actual shooting days to find the "script average," which in this case came to 6.75 pages per day. But by December 11, the actual average was 4.85, prompting a memo from the studio head, Y. Frank Freeman:

"Script totals 162 pages. Daily shooting average has dropped to 4.85. An average of 6.75 is needed to complete picture on a 24 day schedule. We are putting Unit 4 days behind today on the basis of averages, with every indication they will lose additional time."[57] What did it mean to be put behind schedule? Not a lot, but it did indicate to all that the production would probably go over budget, which it did. Principal photography officially closed on January 13, 1954, fifteen days behind schedule and coming in at $262,697 over budget.[58] This clock watching was the primary means by which studios kept costs under control.

While not shot in strict sequence, the filming did follow a rough chronological order, in that earlier scenes were shot early in the filming and later scenes shot later. Most studio productions are shot out of sequence in order to make efficient use of available locations and the cast and crew's time. But with only one set and all the actors signed for the length of the production, it was not necessary to shoot *Rear Window* out of sequence. Hitchcock's extensive preproduction planning ensured that there would not be a lot of wasted film. A couple of interesting shots, however, did not make it into the film in any form. The script originally called for a scene with Ivar Gunnison, the magazine photo editor with whom Jeff talks on the telephone at the beginning of the film.

After the long crane shot over the photographs in Jeff's apartment, which finally ends with the pile of magazines, there was to be a dissolve to a pile of photographs on Gunnison's office desk. There followed a discussion about Indochina ("the next place to watch") between Gunnison (played by Frank Cady, the man on the fire escape, who later became known to television audiences as "Sam Drucker," the grocer from "Green Acres") and his assistant. Gunnison telephones Jeff and they conduct their conversation just as we see it in the film, except that there is a cut-away back to Gunnison once during the talk.[59] Gunnison's office was built on Stage 10 and the scenes were shot, but Hitchcock must have found them superfluous and cut them soon thereafter.[60] It is remarkable that the scenes were in the script in the first place.

On the Cutting-Room Floor: The scene in the photo editor's office, here depicted in a set reference still, was shot but not included in the final version of the film. Frank Cady (right) played Gunnison (misspelled on the slate [far left]). J. Flynn (left) played Bryce, Gunnison's assistant. Photo courtesy of the Academy of Motion Picture Arts and Sciences.

Some scenes in the film (e.g., the opening crane shots) are not within Jeff's point of view and the Gunnison scenes might have fit into this category, but they still violate the single-setting premise of the film. That Hitchcock finally recognized this bode well for the film, if not for Frank Cady.

POSTPRODUCTION AND PUBLICITY

Principal photography ended on January 13, although the crew continued photographing inserts, trailers, and retakes on January 14 and February 4 and 26. Editing began immediately following principal photography, and a final cut was available for musical scoring on March 22. Not slated for VistaVision, Paramount's answer to 20th Century-Fox's CinemaScope, *Rear Window* was shot "flat" and framed for exhibition in Paramount's nonanamorphic "cropped" widescreen process at an aspect ratio of 1.66 to 1.[61] Paramount scheduled the film for a late summer release; it premiered at New York's Rivoli Theater on August 4, 1954, as a benefit for the American–Korean Foundation, which was formed to provide emotional and material relief after the conflict in Asia.[62] The Hollywood premiere occurred on August 11, 1954, at the Hollywood Paramount Theatre.[63] The reviews were almost unanimously ecstatic, with the notable exception of the *New Yorker*, which called the film "claptrap" and its single setting "foolishness."[64] The generally good word of mouth translated into solid box office revenue: at $5.3 million in rentals, it came in fifth for 1954, behind *White Christmas, The Caine Mutiny, The Glenn Miller Story* (another James Stewart vehicle), and *The Egyptian*.[65] It also received four Academy Award nominations – for cinematography, direction, sound recording, and writing – but ultimately did not win any Oscars.

If the "finish work" on the film was complete by the end of spring 1954, the publicity department continued to tinker with the results in its 1954 campaign. Through posters and press kits, this and subsequent campaigns effectively "remodeled" the "structure" of meaning in *Rear Window*. For example, the primary ad mat for Paramount's 1954 campaign features a view of the courtyard from Jeff's apartment, with Jeff in the foreground looking through his telephoto lens. The ad's captions emphasize the "peep show" quality of the film, of course: "The most UNUSUAL and INTIMATE journey into human emotions ever filmed . . . *revealing the privacy of a dozen lives!*" These dozen lives (Miss Torso, Miss Lonely Hearts, The Newlyweds, etc.) are pictured in the apartment windows with appropriate blurbs and exclamation points underneath each character. Significantly, though, the characters have been relocated from their original apartments. The Newlyweds, for example, have been moved to the apartment above Thorwald's, and it appears that the group from the composer's party is two floors above Thorwald. Other ad mats and posters also shuffled the characters around. The three-sheet design places Miss Torso in Thorwald's apartment, Miss Lonely Hearts above her, and the

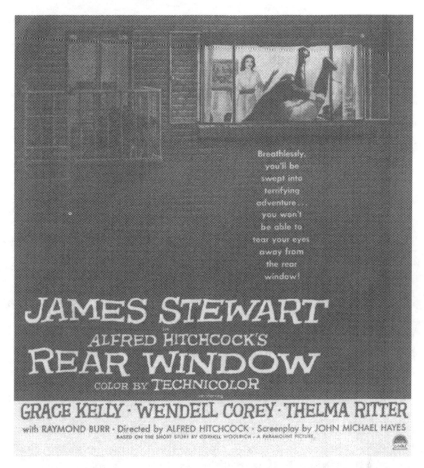

Selling *Rear Window:* An example of the way the publicity department "remodeled" the meaning of the film in the ad campaign (mat 305). Ad courtesy of the Academy of Motion Picture Arts and Sciences.

Newlyweds below. Even more striking is the decision to place Jeff and Lisa in Thorwald's apartment for the six-sheet design and several other smaller ad mats. One ad even depicts Thorwald throwing Jeff out of (or pulling him into) the salesman's apartment as Lisa looks on in her negligee![66] As the ads required simpler and more compact designs, they simplified and sensationalized the complexity of the original space. The construction of meaning continued with the ad campaign, but in a significantly different direction, as we might expect.

But all the ads emphasize the voyeuristic theme of the film, either by depicting Jeff looking (or inviting us to peep) into an open window. When Paramount decided to re-release the film in 1962, they kept this approach. The timing was not fortuitous: The deal that Wasserman and Herman Citron, another of Hitchcock's agents at MCA, had brokered with Paramount required that the studio relinquish the film's rights to Hitchcock after eight years.[67] Any deal that required a studio to give up rights was certainly unusual, but not unheard of. Otto Preminger owned the rights to *The Moon Is Blue* (1953) and *The Man with the Golden Arm* (1956); the rights to several of Cary Grant's films of the late 1950s and early 1960s reverted to him after eight years as well.[68] Hitchcock had the clout at the time he signed with Paramount to demand such considerations. Paramount naturally wanted to squeeze as much out of the film as it could before the deadline passed. The timing was right in another way, as well: the enormous success of *Psycho* (1960) and Hitchcock's high visibility on television's *Alfred Hitchcock Presents* paved the way for another successful publicity campaign.

This time, while emphasizing the voyeurism theme much the same way as before, the ads also relied heavily upon the fame of Hitchcock himself. Hitchcock had been a familiar name in 1954, too, and he had certainly introduced himself to frequent moviegoers with his cameo appearances. But his television series had given him an even greater celebrity and made his profile something of an icon. As with *Psycho,* Hitchcock agreed to promote *Rear Window* through a number of television and radio spots (which was actually quite generous of him since the studio was getting all the revenues for this run).[69] The publicity department recognized and capitalized on his appeal: "The new Hitchcock sell is strongly stressed in the teaser ads, in addition to his being featured in the regular ads and the all-new publicity features. The all-new poster campaign for *Rear Window* has been bolstered with special material keyed to Hitchcock's powerful box-office pull!"[70]

Reselling *Rear Window* in the 1960s: An ad mat from the 1962 campaign, which reused a graphic from the 1954 publicity but added elements to emphasize the success of *Psycho* (1960), Hitchcock's increased familiarity, Burr's new celebrity, and Kelly's royalty (mat 321). Ad courtesy of the Academy of Motion Picture Arts and Sciences.

They emphasized especially Hitchcock's dry wit, which had become an important feature of his television series. The "special material" in the publicity packet included "The Alfred Hitchcock Coloring Book Contest" ("This is Alfred Hitchcock. He is the producer of *Rear Window*. He frightens people to death. He is a nice man. Be kind to him. Color him thin."); radio ads with the master's voice ("If you scream yourself hoarse watching *Rear Window* and cannot tell your friends how much you enjoyed it, please drop them a line."); and the *Rear Window* photo contest ("A tie-in with your local newspaper," reads the manual, "whereby readers are invited to submit photographs taken by themselves from the vantage point of their own 'rear windows.'") The catch line for the campaign was "See it – if your nerves can stand it after *Psycho!*" and the print ads featured Hitchcock's familiar face. (Also notable is the emphasis on Raymond "Perry Mason" Burr in the campaign.) But the famous courtyard set is nowhere to be seen. With this "remodeling," the 1962 campaign relied more on name recognition than curiosity about the story to bring viewers in.

After this successful 1962 run, Hitchcock controlled the film for all future releases. In 1965, he negotiated its broadcast on NBC with the stipulation that it not be edited or cut in any way.[71] According to the contract, NBC planned to show the film twice, once in 1966 and again in 1967 as a "movie special." Hitchcock negotiated a similar agreement with ABC in 1971 and that network broadcast the film the same year. By this time, literary agent Sheldon Abend had acquired the copyright to "It Had to Be Murder," the original short story, and filed suit against Hitchcock and Stewart in 1974 for copyright infringement.[72] Abend eventually settled out of court for $25,000.[73] But it was not the threat of a lawsuit that kept Hitchcock from releasing *Rear Window* again. Citron would cite only "personal reasons" for this decision, but Hitchcock might have wanted to create demand and save any future profits for his heirs; in a way, *Rear Window* and the other films might have acted as a trust fund.[74]

So it was only after Hitchcock's death in 1980, and the death in 1982 of his wife, Alma, that the re-release of *Rear Window* and four other films (*Rope, The Man Who Knew Too Much, The Trouble with Harry,* and *Vertigo*) once again became a possibility. In April 1983, Universal announced that it had licensed worldwide rights for these films in all media from the Hitchcock estate.[75] *Rear Window,* the first of the re-releases, did extraordinary business for a thirty-year-old revival: Upon its opening, it broke one-day box office records for art houses around the country[76] and ended up pulling in $6.8 million in its first five months.[77] The success of the film

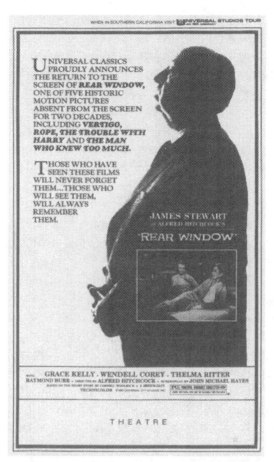

Reselling *Rear Window* in the 1980s: An ad mat from the 1983 campaign emphasizes the film as part of a package of rarely seen classics of Hitchcock thrillers. Ad courtesy of the Academy of Motion Picture Arts and Sciences.

was tarnished only by the announcement in April 1984 of another lawsuit by Abend, again contending copyright infringement.[78] This one would take six years to resolve, the Supreme Court finally deciding in Abend's favor.

Universal once again "remodeled" the film for its re-release. In one particularly egregious example, they cut out the last shot of the film – Jeff's curtains closing on the courtyard – in order to replace the Paramount logo with their own, thus erasing the final segment of the narrative's circular and reflexive pattern. The film's themes and design received scant attention in the ad campaign as well. Relying primarily upon Hitchcock's name and recognizability – with the popularity of the *auteur* theory in the 1970s, Hitchcock's cultural capital had skyrocketed – Universal designed only one graphic for all the posters and print ads and ignored the courtyard set except in the press releases. The posters for each of the re-released films included one scene still from the respective production; for *Rear Window,* the shot depicted Jeff and Lisa lounging in his apartment, not even looking out the window. Nostalgia, romance, and celebrity had replaced the courtyard, voyeurism, and sensationalism as the primary structures of meaning in the ad campaign.

Yet Hitchcock's imprimatur was clearly visible, even overshadowing his construction. During the 1960s, Hitchcock's growing fame as the host of *Alfred Hitchcock Presents* contributed to the shift in focus in the ad campaigns from the set to the director. By the 1980s, his stature as an *auteur* was assured and the publicity campaign for the five re-released films reflected this: Hitchcock's rotund profile is the dominant graphic for the posters for all five films. By 1983, then, Hitchcock had become, just as the *Rear Window* courtyard had once been, the biggest thing since Cecil B. DeMille.

NOTES

Abbreviations in Notes

AHC	Alfred Hitchcock Collection
CC	Core Collection production clipping file: *Rear Window*
MPAA/PCA	Motion Picture Association of America/Production Code Administration Files: *Rear Window*
PA – Press.	Paramount Collection – Press Books: *Rear Window*
PA – Prod.	Paramount Collection – Production Records: *Rear Window*
PA – Scr.	Paramount Collection – Scripts: *Rear Window*

All collections are located at the Academy of Motion Picture Arts and Sciences' Margaret Herrick Library in Beverly Hills, California.

I would like to thank Val Almendarez, Jennifer Barker, and especially John Belton for their insightful comments on a earlier draft of this chapter.

1. "Detail Production Cost," January 24, 1956, PA – Prod. This calculation does not include Stewart, who deferred his salary for a percentage of the profits.
2. Arthur E. Gavin, "Rear Window," *American Cinematographer* 35, No. 2 (February 1954), 97.
3. See especially Jean Douchet, "Hitch and His Public," *A Hitchcock Reader,* ed. Marshall Deutelbaum and Leland Poague (Ames: Iowa State University Press, 1986), 7–15; and Robert Stam and Roberta Pearson, "Hitchcock's *Rear Window:* Reflexivity and the Critique of Voyeurism," *A Hitchcock Reader,* 193–206.
4. John Belton, "The Space of *Rear Window,*" *Modern Language Notes* 103. No. 5 (December 1989), 1122.
5. Michael R. Diliberto, "Looking through the 'Rear Window': A Review of the United States Supreme Court Decision in *Stewart v. Abend,*" *Loyola of Los Angeles Entertainment Law Journal* 12, No. 2 (1992), 299. See also *Stewart v. Abend,* 495 U.S. 207 (1990).
6. Paramount story summary, November 17, 1944, PA – Scr.
7. Diliberto, 299.
8. A friend brought this book and the impending sale to Hitchcock's attention in 1950, but apparently Hitchcock was either too occupied or not interested and let the opportunity pass. See Daniel M. Winkler to Alfred Hitchcock, December 18, 1950, box 107, folder 1309, AHC. My thanks to Val Almendarez for bringing this letter to my attention.
9. A treatment is an intermediate step between the story and the finished screenplay; it usually consists of a narrative containing all the principal situations and may include some dialogue or description of the settings.
10. Joshua Logan, *Movie Stars, Real People, and Me* (New York: Delacorte Press, 1978), 241.
11. See Logan treatment and accompanying letter from Kathleen Malley (Hayward's secretary) to Wasserman, dated April 20, 1953, box 52, folders 615 and 617, AHC. Logan's plan to direct *Mister Roberts* soon ran aground, too; John Ford and Mervyn LeRoy shared directing credit for the 1955 Warner Bros. film.
12. The agreement with Paramount called for Hitchcock to produce, direct, and eventually own all rights to five films (they turned out to be *Rear Window, The Trouble with Harry, The Man Who Knew Too Much, Vertigo,* and *Psycho*) and for Paramount to produce and own four (the studio ended up owning only one, *To Catch a Thief*). Donald Spoto, *The Dark Side of Genius: The Life of Alfred Hitchcock* (Boston: Little, Brown and Co., 1983), 344.
13. "Simplest Explanation," *New York Times,* May 3, 1953, CC. See also "Logan, Hayward, Stewart, Hitchcock's WB Indie," *Variety* 191, No. 7 (July 22, 1953), 3, which incorrectly lists it as a Warner Bros. film.

14. Hitchcock was certainly familiar with Woolrich's work before encountering this particular story. Joan Harrison, one of Hollywood's first female producers, had been Hitchcock's longtime personal assistant and friend before moving on to produce *Phantom Lady* (Universal, 1944) from a Woolrich novel. Shortly after *Rear Window*'s release, Harrison worked with Hitchcock again as associate producer of his long-running television series *Alfred Hitchcock Presents*, which adapted three Woolrich stories: "The Big Switch" (broadcast January 8, 1956), "Momentum" (broadcast June 24, 1956), and "Post Mortem" (broadcast May 18, 1958).

15. "Story, Scenario, Producer and Director" budget sheet, November 14, 1953, PA – Prod.

16. "Legal Notes Relative to Haygan Incorporated – 'Rear Window,'" October 1, 1953, PA – Prod. Unfortunately, the exact details of Hitchcock and Stewart's contract with Paramount are not a matter of public record.

17. Hayward received a special nod in the film as well; during Lisa Fremont's first scene with Jefferies, she describes her day: "Then I had to have a cocktail with Leland and Slim Hayward; we're trying to get his show." Incidentally, the wine bucket, dinner plates, and napkins brought by the waiter in that scene were flown in from the actual 21 Club in New York. They even flew in the waiter's jacket with a photograph of an actual waiter wearing it (in order to match the rest of the costume). See [Frank] Caffey to [Russell] Holman, transcripts of telegrams dated November 7 and 25, 1953, PA – Prod.

18. Warner Bros. "Memorandum of Daily Production Costs – Summary" for *Dial M for Murder*, PA – Prod.

19. Spoto, 344.

20. Spoto, 345.

21. John Michael Hayes, "Setting the Record Straight: Screenwriter John Michael Hayes Talks about Hollywood and Hitchcock," *Columbia Film View* 8, No. 1 (Winter/Spring 1990), 8.

22. List of scenario completion dates, PA – Prod.

23. List of scenario completion dates, PA – Prod.

24. "Production Budget," October 8 and November 30, 1953, PA – Prod.

25. Hayes 8.

26. See Ronald Haver, *David O. Selznick's Hollywood* (New York: Knopf, 1980), 246; and Alan David Vertrees, "Reconstructing the 'Script in Sketch Form': An Analysis of the Narrative Construction and Production Design of the Fire Sequence in *Gone with the Wind*," *Film History* 3, No. 2 (1989), 87–104. Haver maintains that storyboards had always been standard procedure for animated films and special-effects sequences, and that Selznick's use of a storyboard for an entire feature was innovative. Certain modern directors, notably Steven Spielberg and Martin Scorsese, have revived the practice as a

means of cutting costs and ensuring authorial control. See Scott Busby, "Imagining Movies," *Premiere* 2, No. 11 (July 1989), 68–73.

27. Budge Crawley, Fletcher Markle, and Gerald Pratley, "I Wish I Didn't Have to Shoot the Picture: An Interview with Alfred Hitchcock," *Focus on Hitchcock*, ed. Albert LaValley (Englewood Cliffs, NJ: Prentice-Hall, 1972), 25.

28. John M. Woodcock, A.C.E., "The Name Dropper: Alfred Hitchcock," *American Cinemeditor* 40, No. 2 (Summer 1990), 36.

29. Woodcock, 37.

30. Belton, "Space," 1126–1128.

31. Mac Johnson to C. O. Erickson, October 5, 1953, PA – Prod. In the film, Thorwald lives at 125 W. 9th, but there is nothing in the records to indicate that the research team used that specific location, though they may have photographed courtyards in this area. Hitchcock also requested, a month later, tape recordings of sounds from Greenwich Village, especially from street corners at various times of day. See [Frank] Caffey to [Russell] Holman, transcript of telegram dated November 6, 1953, PA – Prod. The skill of the sound recording earned Harry Lindgren (the mixer), John Cope (his assistant), and Loren Ryder (the department head) an Academy Award nomination.

32. "Summary of approved set estimates including supplements," and daily camera report, November 13, 1953, PA – Prod.

33. Universal News production notes, August 17, 1983, CC.

34. Paramount production notes, 1954, CC.

35. "Detail Production Cost," January 24, 1956, PA – Prod.

36. Paramount production notes, 1954, CC.

37. Gavin, 97.

38. Gavin, 97.

39. David Atkinson, "Hitchcock's Techniques Tell *Rear Window* Story," *American Cinematographer* 71, No. 1 (January 1990), 37–38.

40. "Analysis of Costs of Scenario, Supervision, Direction and Cast," accompanying "Detail Production Cost," September 4, 1954, PA – Prod. Unless they had made other arrangements or were day workers, most actors had a weekly rate. The total number of days they spent with the production was divided by a six-day week; this figure was then multiplied by their rate to come up with the final pay. Ritter worked for 37 days at $4,166.67 a week. Grace Kelly worked for 50 days at $2,857.15 per week. Wendell Corey spent 51 days on the set at $2,500 per week. And Raymond Burr worked 41 days at $1,250 a week. Because Stewart and Hitchcock deferred their salaries, their paychecks do not show up in the cost analyses. They took home a percentage of the $200,000 mentioned above, but exact figures unfortunately are unavailable.

41. John Belton, *Cinema Stylists* (Metuchen, NJ: Scarecrow Press, 1983), 16.

42. List of scenario completion dates, PA – Prod.
43. Joseph Breen to Luigi Luraschi, November 20, 1953, MPAA/PCA.
44. "Memo for the files," November 27, 1953, MPAA/PCA.
45. My thanks to Barbara Hall for this insight, which can be found in an interesting discussion of Breen office practices with a longtime member of the Production Code staff: "An Oral History with Albert E. Van Schmus," interviewed by Barbara Hall, Oral History Program, AMPAS, 1993, 346–348.
46. Lowell E. Redelings, "The Hollywood Scene," *Hollywood Citizen-News*, July 19, 1954, CC; Universal News production notes, August 17, 1983, CC; Belton, *Cinema Stylists*, 16.
47. Atkinson, 37–38.
48. The most famous of these arguments is Laura Mulvey's "Visual Pleasure and Narrative Cinema," *Screen* 16.3 (1975), 6–18. For answers to this seminal article, cf. William Rothman, *Hitchcock – The Murderous Gaze* (Cambridge, MA: Harvard University Press, 1982), or Marian E. Keane, "A Closer Look at Scopophilia: Mulvey, Hitchcock, and *Vertigo*," *A Hitchcock Reader*, 231–248.
49. Belton, *Cinema Stylists*, 15–16.
50. Gavin, 78.
51. Atkinson, 37–38.
52. Jonathan Coe, *Jimmy Stewart: A Wonderful Life* (New York: Arcade Publishing, 1994), 140–142. See also Redelings, "The Hollywood Scene."
53. Atkinson, 39.
54. Gavin, 77.
55. Daily camera reports, January 11, 1954 (Setup #12) and February 4, 1954 (Setup #10), PA – Prod.
56. The scene in which Thorwald picks up Jeff and starts to throw him out the window caused some problems for the actors: Ted Mapes, Stewart's double, sliced open his right thigh as he slid out the window, and Raymond Burr strained his back picking up Mapes. "Personal Injury Report" for Burr, January 7, 1954; "Personal Injury Report" for Mapes, January 11, 1954, PA – Prod. (The bill for Burr's treatment on the set came to $15! See "Check Requisition" for Dr. Francis Abdo, January 15, 1954, PA – Prod.)
57. "Daily Production Report," December 11, 1953, PA – Prod.
58. "Detail Production Cost," January 24, 1956, PA – Prod. Total cost came to $1,137,697.
59. Final white script, December 1, 1953, 4–10, PA – Scr.
60. Daily camera reports, January 13, 1954 (Setups #12–13); February 4, 1954 (Setup #7), PA – Prod.
61. VistaVision made its premiere with *White Christmas*, which was shot from mid-August to December 1953, approximately the same time as *Rear Window*. It could be that, after his frustrating experi-

ence with 3-D during *Dial M for Murder,* Hitchcock decided against trying out another new technology.

62. Spoto, 353.

63. Edwin Schallert, "Hitchcock Razzle-Dazzles at Brilliant Premiere," *Los Angeles Times;* and Lowell E. Redelings, "*Rear Window* Melodrama Delights Premiere Crowd," *Hollywood Citizen-News,* August 12, 1954, CC.

64. John McCarten, "The Current Cinema: Hitchcock Confined Again," *New Yorker,* August 7, 1954, CC.

65. "1954 Box Office Champs," *Variety* 197, No. 5 (January 5, 1955), 59. "Rentals" indicate the distributor's share; "gross" refers to the total dollar amount taken in, which includes the exhibitor's percentage.

66. All these ads are pictured in the Paramount Showmanship Manual, release season 1954–1955, group A-14, PA – Press.

67. Aljean Harmetz, "Hitchcock's Death May 'Revive' 5 Films," *New York Times,* July 9, 1980, CC.

68. It is only fair to note that because United Artists, through which Preminger released his films, relied upon independently produced films, it cut different deals than the other major studios.

69. See also letters to Hitchcock from Martin S. Davis, Paramount's director of advertising, publicity and exploitation, box 52, folder 618, AHC. Unfortunately, *Rear Window* did not show up on *Variety's* 1962 year-end rental chart, and box office grosses were not reported consistently at this time, so revenue figures are unavailable.

70. Paramount Showmanship Manual, release season 1962–1963, group A-22, 4, PA – Press.

71. "Hitchcock Wants No Cuts in *Rear Window* on TV," *The Hollywood Reporter* 188, No. 30 (December 14, 1965), 2.

72. "Owner of Copyright for Basic *Rear Window* Pic Story Asks $2 Million over Telecasting," *Daily Variety* 163, No. 62 (May 31, 1974), 1, 14.

73. Diliberto, 300.

74. Harmetz, "Hitchcock's Death May 'Revive' 5 Films."

75. "Uni to Return 5 Classic Hitchcock Films to Public Eye," *The Hollywood Reporter* 276.31 (April 11, 1983), 1, 6; and "Universal Acquires Five Hitchcock Pix," *Daily Variety* 199, No. 35 (April 22, 1983), 2.

76. "*Rear Window* Breaks Records at 3 Theaters," *New York Times,* October 6, 1983, CC.

77. Richard Corliss, "The Master Who Knew Too Much," *Time* (March 26, 1954), 77.

78. "C'right Violations Charged in *Rear Window* Reissue Suit," *Daily Variety* 203, No. 32 (April 18, 1984), 1, 20.

WIDESCREEN – EASTMAN COLOR – STEREOPHONIC SOUND — Sheet No. 1

Release Season _____
Starting Date __November 27, 1953__
Finishing Date __December 24, 1953__
Camera Days __24__

PARAMOUNT PICTURES CORPORATION
5451 MARATHON ST.
HOLLYWOOD 38, CALIFORNIA
PRODUCTION BUDGET

Production No. __10331__
Producer __Alfred Hitchcock__
Director __Alfred Hitchcock__
Working Title __Rear Window__

Acct. No.	DESCRIPTION		Sheet Ref.	ACTUAL COST TO 11/14	ESTIMATED COST TO COMPLETE	TOTAL BUDGET	ABOVE THE LINE CHARGES	BELOW THE LINE CHARGES Physical & Shooting	Editing
201	Story:	Rights	2	25,000.	–	25,000.	25,000.		
211	Scenario:	Writers	2	17,250.	1,500.	18,750.	18,750.		
212		Miscellaneous	2	617.	1,183.	1,800.	1,800.		
220	Producer and Staff		2	–	–	–	Exclusive		
231	Direction:	Director and Staff	2	100.	–	100.	Exclusive	100.	
232		Technical Staff	10	–	5,366.	5,366.	2,000.	3,166.	200.
233-4		Dance Staff & Rehearsal Expense	10	–	600.	600.		600.	
241	Players:	Cast	3	221.	99,265.	99,486.	96,273.	2,763.	450.
242		Extras	4	266.	4,956.	5,222.		4,972.	250.
251	Wardrobe:	Designing	5	2.	1,298.	1,300.		1,300.	
252		Purchased or Manufactured	5	–	6,900.	6,900.		6,900.	
253		Rented	5	–	630.	630.		630.	
254		Maintenance	5	–	800.	800.		800.	
260	Makeup and Hairdressing Materials		10	–	500.	500.		500.	
271-4	Nursery		8	916.	3,284.	4,200.		4,200.	
281-3	Action Props		6	746.	8,619.	9,365.		9,365.	
290	Lighting		7	9,798.	55,202.	65,000.		65,000.	
301	Set Dressing: Interior Decorators		11	266.	1,434.	1,700.		1,700.	
302-6		Set Dressings	8	2,948.	7,752.	10,700.		10,700.	
311	Sets:	Designing	11	6,078.	2,732.	8,810.		8,810.	
12		Construction	8	66,284.	5,716.	72,000.		72,000.	
		Striking	8	7,413.	867.	8,280.		8,280.	
		Moving and Re-setting Sets	8	–	–	–			
		Operation	11	12,885.	41,615.	54,500.		54,500.	
		General Effects	8	250.	3,525.	3,775.		3,775.	
	Miniatures:	Construction	8	–	–	–			
		Action Props	8	–	–	–			
		Operation and Striking	8	–	–	–			
	Transparencies		8	–	–	–			
	Locations		9	–	–	–			
	Operating Staffs: Production		10	2,687.	6,583.	9,270.		9,270.	
		Wardrobe	10	–	2,968.	2,968.		2,968.	
		Property	10	520.	3,166.	3,686.		3,686.	
		Makeup and Hairdressing	10	–	3,980.	3,980.		3,980.	
		Cameramen	11	166.	11,625.	11,791.		11,791.	
	Camera Rentals		11	487.	3,513.	4,000.		4,000.	
	General Transportation		11	5,008.	3,792.	8,800.	1,500.	6,800.	500.
	Music		12	–	41,830.	41,830.			41,830.
	Sound Recording		12	–	20,430.	20,430.		9,940.	10,490.
	Editing:	Cutting and Projectionists	13	396.	18,275.	18,671.		4,930.	13,741.
	Titles and Miscellaneous Effects		8	–	7,100.	7,100.		7,100.	
430	Negative Film		13	–	25,052.	25,052.		14,080.	10,972.
440	Positive Film		13	–	31,044.	31,044.		6,280.	24,764.
450	Living Expense		13	33.	1,467.	1,500.	200.	840.	460.
460	Insurance and Taxes		13	1,804.	27,196.	29,000.	20,000.	8,362.	638.
470	Salaries: Pending Approval & Earned Vacations		13	3,020.	7,150.	10,170.		9,547.	623.
480	Miscellaneous and Tests		13	1,794.	17,257.	19,051.		16,651.	2,400.
	Sound Recording Royalties & Ascap Royalties		13	818.	6,432.	7,250.	4,750.	2,310.	190.
	Total Direct Costs			167,773.	492,604.	660,377.	170,273.	382,596.	107,508.
490	Overhead 32.5 % of Direct Costs		13	54,527.	160,096.	214,623.	55,339.	124,344.	34,940.
							NOTE: Figure is exclusive of Producer, Director, portion of Story Rights and James Stewart.		
	GRAND TOTALS			222,300.	652,700.	875,000.	225,612.	506,940.	142,448.

ACTUAL TIME

Date Started __November 27, 1953__ Days — Production _____
Date Completed _____ Days — Retakes, etc. _____
Total Days: _____
Release Title _____

BUDGET AND STORY CERTIFICATIONS

Compiled from: __167 page complete yellow script dated__
__October 20, 1953 thru November 30, 1953 by John__
__Michael Hayes__

Compiled by: Date __November 30, 1953__ Approved _____
Approved _____
Approved _____ Approved _____
Approved _____ Approved _____

PRINCIPAL PLAYERS

James Stewart   Grace Kelly
Wendell Corey   Thelma Ritter

10331 – REAR WINDOW

The budget for *Rear Window*, dated November 30, 1953.

PARAMOUNT PICTURES CORPORATION
west coast studios

Producer ALFRED HITCHCOCK
Director ALFRED HITCHCOCK
Principal Players J. STEWART, G. KELLY, W. COREY, T. RITTER
Budget | 24 | Day Schedule $ 875,000.00

DETAIL PRODUCTION COST

PATRON, INC.

Production No. 10311   Class A
Release Title "REAR WINDOW" (Widescreen)
From Story: Eastman, Stereo, Sound)
Budget 262,697.05   (See Reverse Side)

Cost $ 1,137,697.05

No.	Item	COSTS Paramount	Patron	COMBINED TO DATE		No.	Item	COSTS Paramount	Patron	COMBINED TO DATE
201	STORY RIGHTS		25,000.00	25,000.00		351	OPERATING STAFFS — Production	16,818.84		16,818.84
211	SCENARIO — Writers		19,125.00	19,125.00		352	— Wardrobe	2,935.92		2,935.92
212	— Miscellaneous	1,297.26	78.75	1,376.01		353	— Property	5,641.91		5,641.91
220	PRODUCER AND STAFF					354	— Makeup and Hairdressing	6,843.24		6,843.24
231	DIRECTION — Director and Staff	4,350.00		4,350.00		355	— Camera	18,454.77		18,454.77
232	— Technical Staff	7,356.72		7,356.72		360	CAMERA RENTALS	9,256.98		9,256.98
233	— Dance Director and Staff	800.00		800.00		371	TRANSPORTATION — Autos and Trucks	10,201.55		10,201.55
234	— Dance Rehearsal Expense	9.90		9.90		372	— Other	1,903.53	111.64	2,015.17
241	PLAYERS — Cast	18,778.18	104,557.62	123,335.80		381	MUSIC — Rights	3,535.20	1,350.00	4,885.20
242	— Extras	13,602.62		13,602.62		382	— Preparation	7,457.89	12,500.00	19,957.89
251	WARDROBE — Designing	1,209.34		1,209.34		383	— Scoring	26,347.12		26,347.12
252	— Purchased and Mfg.	6,312.44		6,312.44		391	SOUND RECORDING — Shooting	16,966.08		16,966.08
253	— Rented	57.00		57.00		392	— Sound Effects	3,933.44		3,933.44
254	— Maintenance	993.41		993.41		393	— Scoring	3,620.00		3,620.00
260	MAKEUP AND HAIRDRESSING	1,374.76		1,374.76		394	— Dubbing	6,552.20		6,552.20
271	NURSERY — Purchased, Mfg. or Rented	2,097.31		2,097.31		401	EDITING AND SUPERVISION	10,693.47		10,693.47
272	— Installing	660.54		660.54		402	— Projection	6,393.78		6,393.78
273	— Oper. and Maintenance	2,240.10		2,240.10		403	— Stock Shots	91.00		91.00
274	— Striking	292.08		292.08		404	— Effects Editing	4,066.16		4,066.16
281	ACTION PROPS — Purchased and Mfg.	5,452.85		5,452.85		405	— Music Editing	2,569.65		2,569.65
282	— Rented	4,717.35		4,717.35		410	TITLES AND MISC. EFFECTS	8,801.59		8,801.59
283	— Oper. and Maintenance	3,077.69		3,077.69		421	NEGATIVE FILM — Picture	14,394.06		14,394.06
291	LIGHTING — Equipment Rentals	24,496.45		24,496.45		422	— Sound	9,109.36		9,109.36
292	— Rigging and Striking	5,963.61		5,963.61		423	— Lab. Expense	5,592.30		5,592.30
293	— Operation	65,303.24		65,303.24		424	— Neg. Cutters	965.48		965.48
301	SET DRESSING — Set Dressers	1,941.30		1,941.30		430	POSITIVE FILM AND LAB. EXPENSE	34,949.12		34,949.12
302	— Purchased or Mfg.	4,302.36		4,302.36		440	LIVING EXPENSE	2,542.73		2,542.73
303	— Rented	1,115.11		1,115.11		450	INSURANCE AND TAXES	9,397.01	38,359.45	47,756.46
304	— Installing	2,813.24		2,813.24		460	RETROACTIVE WAGE ADJ.	9,139.83		9,139.83
305	— Maintenance and Oper.	3,451.04		3,451.04		461	PROV. FOR EARNED VACATIONS	11,518.48		11,518.48
306	— Striking	621.15		621.15		470	MISC. EXPENSE	8,843.46	610.07	9,453.53
311	SETS — Designing	9,285.19		9,285.19		471	TESTS	13,311.68		13,311.68
312	— Construction	72,505.19		72,505.19		480	SOUND RECORDING ROYALTIES	1,512.00		1,512.00
314	— Striking	7,577.60		7,577.60		482	ASCAP PERFORMANCE FEE	3,975.00		3,975.00
315	— Moving and Resetting					485	Welfare Contribution	3,689.44		3,689.44
316	— Oper. and Maintenance						TOTAL DIRECT CHARGES	661,048.41	201,692.53	862,740.94
317	— General Effects					490	OVERHEAD 30% =304,765.80	75,242.99	16,186.75	91,429.74
321	MINIATURES — Construction					490	O.H. 32.5% =549,629.15	130,615.04	48,014.43	178,629.47
324	— Action Props					490	O.H. 28% =710,346.01	2,896.88		2,896.88
325	— Oper. and Maintenance						TOTAL PRODUCTION COST	871,803.34	265,893.71	1,137,697.05
330	TRANSPARENCIES	910.91		910.91						
341	LOCATIONS — Survey						FILM FOOTAGE AND SHOOTING SCHEDULE			
342	— Staff						NEGATIVE PICTURE FILM	119,730		
343	— Fees						NEGATIVE SOUND FILM	318,662		
344	— Living Expense						POSITIVE FILM	251,154		
345	— Transportation	7.32		7.32			TOTAL FILM	689,546		
346	— Misc. Expense	108.64		108.64						

DATE STARTED 11-27-53
DATE COMPLETED 1-13-54
CAMERA DAYS 39
RETAKE DAYS 1

DATE ISSUED: 1-24-56
COST TO: 12-31-55

CERTIFIED CORRECT
PREPARED BY:
APPROVED

A detail production cost sheet for *Rear Window*, dated January 24, 1955.

53

PRODUCTION _____ REAR WINDOW _____ No. 10331

~~EXT NEWLYWED'S WINDOW~~ _____ DATE SHOT __1-13-54__

SETUP No.	TAKES MADE	SLATES PRINTED	TIME FIRST SETUP GIVEN	TIME CAMERA READY	TIME FIRST TAKE	TIME SCENE COMPLETED	DESCRIPTION OF ANGLES, ACTION AND DIALOGUE
1	1	473-1	1/12	9.00	9.13 (30)		189: Ext. NEWLYWED'S WINDOW: Boy puts blind up, looks out, hears wife's voice call him, pulls shade down. (pajamas & undershirt on)
1A	1	HOLD 474-1				9.30	189 – ALTERNATE. Same as Scene 473, except that boy wears trousers instead of pajamas.
2	3	HOLD 475-3	9.32	9.45	9.52		252- ALTERNATE. 2" M.S. at Newlywed's window. Shadow on blind shows boy lighting cigaret; he puts blind up, looks out; her voice calls him; he throws cigaret down and pulls down blind. (Trousers & undershirt on)
2A	1	476-1			(21)	10.00	252: Same as Scene 473 above, except the he wears pajamas instead of trousers.
3	3	477-3	10.01	10.04	10.05 (10)	10.10	2" M.S. of Newlywed's Window, with shade down and light on inside.
4	3	478-3	10.15	10.42	10.48 (15)	11.00	319-332: 2" M.S. to Newlyweds' Window; shade goes up, disclosing boy and girl in night clothes; they look off rt. as if at woman yelling about dog being killed; go back in and close shade.
4A	1	HOLD 479-1				11.12	319-332: Same as 478 above, except that boy has trousers on instead of pajamas, and girl has dress on instead of negligee.
5	1	480-1	11.15	11.48	11.52 (10)	11.55	2 & 479C: 2" M.S. shooting up to Newlywed's window; shade is raised and they look off as if at Jeff when he is hanging from window sill.
5A	1	481-1			(7)	11.55	479C: 2" M.S. up to Newlyweds in window as they look down as if when Jeff is on ground after fall from window.
6	2	482-2	12.00 Lunch 12.00	1.18	1.23 (10)	1.28	65: 2" MLS to Song Writer's Apartment; he is playing piano, while man in b.g. (Hitchcock) winds up clock on mantel.
7	1	483-1	1.31	1.52	1.56 (20)	1.57	384: 2" MLS to Song Writer's Apt. – he is seated at piano, playing, while around him other musicians, with guitar, harmonica, trumpet and clarinet try out their parts.
8	3	484-3	1.58	2.01	2.02 (27)	2.20	404: 2" MLS to Song Writer's apt., as he and four other musicians play his composition.
9	1	485-1	2.22	2.29	2.30 (7)	2.31	479-D: 2" M.S. to Songwriter's Apt., showing Song Writer and four musicians looking down as if when Jeff is on ground.

cont'd....

(continued)

PRODUCTION _____ REAR WINDOW _____ No. __1-331__

EXT. SONG WRITERS' APT & NEWLYWEDS - INT. _____ DATE SHOT __1-13-54__
   GUNNISSONS' OFFICE

SETUP No.	TAKES MADE	SLATES PRINTED	TIME FIRST SETUP GIVEN	TIME CAMERA READY	TIME FIRST TAKE	TIME SCENE COMPLETED	DESCRIPTION OF ANGLES, ACTION AND DIALOGUE
						Page Two	
10	1	486X-1	2.32	2.38	2.40	2.41	TRAILER - 5C: 2" M.S. to Song Writer's Apt.; he is playing piano.
11	2	487-2	2.45	2.52	2.56	2.59	TRAILER - 5A: 2" M.S. to Newlywed's Window, showing them arguing.
12	1	488-1	3.05	3.28	3.40 (54)	3.41	2: Int. GUNNISON'S OFFICE; 40MM M.S. Gunnison at desk, with Bryce standing near. They discuss sending someone to Indo-China; Gunnison takes up one and calls Jeffries and talks to him as in Script Sc. 2 to where he says "Seven weeks since you broke your leg - yes or no?"
13	4	489-4	3.44	3.52	3.55	4.11	3A, 6, 11A, 15E, 15A; INT GUNNISONS OFFICE; 60MM C.S. Gunnison with phone as he talks to Jeff, from where he says "Congratulations, Jeff", thru to "You know best, Jeff. I'll call you later"; he puts phone down.
14	1	490X-1	4.20	5.00	5.05	5.07	347A-349A-351A: Int. Jeff's Apt.: TRICK SHOT TO BE FINISHED BY FULTON. Camera shooting down to flower bed, for effect of comparing slide with actual condition of flower bed.
15	1 (Sound Track called 490-1)	491-1	5.15	5.50	5.57	5.58	110 RETAKE: 2" MLS SongWriter enters his apartment, drunk, staggers around, throws music off piano, and falls into chair.

SCENES: 59,187,189,258,319,352,404,
     2, 6.
Finish 478; Retakes 65,110.
Trailer Scens 5A & 5C.
S.P.D. Part 347,349,351.

Pages: 3-1/4

Daily camera report for *Rear Window*, dated January 13, 1954, which includes the Gunnison scene.

DAILY PRODUCTION REPORT F   PRODUCTION___10331 - REAR WINDOW - EAST___

Producer___A HITCHCOCK___Director___A HITCHCOCK___Cameraman___R BURKS___Date___January 13___19_54_

Date Started___11/27/53___   Schedule Finishing Date___12/24/53___ Schedule Days___24___

Camera Days to Date___39___   Indicated Finishing Date___1/13/54___ Status___15 DAYS BEHIND & 2 HOLS___

Name of Set	Set No.	Location or Stage	Diffused Yes	Diffused No
EXT NEIGHBORHOOD AND COURTYARD	1	STAGE 18		x
INT GUNNISON'S OFFICE	2	STAGE 10		x
TRAILER SHOTS	1	STAGE 18		x
EXT NEIGHBORHOOD AND COURTYARD	1	STAGE 18		x

Company Called___9:00 AM

Camera Called 8:00 AM Sound Called 8:00 AM

Lining Up & Rehearsing 9:00 AM TO 9:12 AM

1st Shot 9:12 AM

Lunch: From 11:58 AM To 12:58 PM

Lining Up & Rehearsing 12:58 PM TO 1:23 PM

1st Shot 1:23 PM

Dinner: From___To___

Lining Up & Rehearsing___

1st Shot___

Company Finished 6:02 PM

Camera Finished 6:02 PM Sound Finished 6:02 PM

Total Pages	162	Script Avg.	6.75	
Taken Prev.	157¼			
Taken Today	3¼ & ½ RTKS			
Total To Date	161	Actual Average	4.13	
Added				2
Elim.				2
		Rtks.		½
Pre-Prod.		Taken to Date	5¾	
2nd Unit				
Inserts Stk. etc.		Time on Rtks.	12 HRS	
To Be Taken	1		15 MIN	

	Picture Negative			Magnetic Film
	1st Unit	Good	Waste	Good
Prev.	92145	7055	78585	
Today	1990	80	1990	
To Date	94135	7135	80575	
2nd Unit To Date				
Total To Date				

Music

Song or Number:

Playback Track No.___Dir. Recording___

Photography

No. Camera Set-Ups 15 No. Cameras 2 Effect EASTMAN COLOR-SPD Boom No.___

Script Scenes Taken

Remarks and Reasons for Delay

MOVED FROM STG 18 TO STG 10 3:00 PM - MOVED FROM STG 10 TO STG 18 4:15 PM.

✓ PRODUCTION CLOSED 1/13/54.

2-6-59-187-189-252-319-332-404
478 (FINISH)
SPD: 347 (PART)-349-351
TRAILER: 5a-5c
RETAKES: 65-110
TOTAL SCRIPT__14__ ADDED__0__ RETAKES__2__

	CAST	CHARACTER	1st CALL	TIME CALLED SET	TIME FINISHED	CONTRACT START	CONTRACT FINISH	PICTURE START	PICTURE FINISH	USED	IDLE	ILL	Rhsl	B'cast
1	J STEWART	JEFF				PICTURE		11/27	1/9	28	8			
2	G KELLY	LISA				11/16	1/2	12/3	1/12	25	23			
3	R BURR	SALESMAN				11/27	12/24	11/27	1/12	25	12	1		
4	I WINSTON	MRS THORWALD				DAILY		11/27	11/28	2				
5	T RITTER	STELLA				11/30	1/9	11/30	1/11	22	13			
6	W COREY	DOYLE				11/12	1/6	11/30	1/11	11	39			
7	G DARCY	TORSO				11/24	12/21	11/27	1/12	34	5			2
8	J EVELYN	LONELY HEART				12/8	12/28	12/14	1/12	19	10			
9	R BAGDASARIAN	SONGWRITER	9:00A	9:00A	6:02P	11/27	12/24	11/27	1/13	35	4			
10	J LANSING	SUNBATHERS				12/14	1/9	12/14	12/15	2				
	S CASEY					DAILY		12/16	12/16	1				
	(Conv to WKLY)					12/17	12/23	12/17	1/12	16	5			
11	S GRIFFIN					12/14	1/9	12/14	12/15	2				
	J PARIS					DAILY		12/16	12/16	1				
	(Conv to WKLY)					12/17	12/23	12/17	1/8	14	4			
12	R HARPER	HONEYMOONERS	8:00A	9:00A	3:30P	STOCK		1/9	1/13	4				
13	H DAVENPORT		7:30A	9:00A	3:30P	DAILY		1/9	1/13	4				
17	F CADY	FIRE ESCAPE				11/24	12/21	11/27	1/12	30	11			
	S BERNER	COUPLE				11/27	12/17	11/27	1/12	30	8			
18	I CASTIGLIONI	BIRDWOMAN				DAILY		11/27	11/28	2				
19	F CADY	GUNNISON	10:00A	10:00A	4:00P	DAILY		1/13	1/13	1				
20	J FLYNN	BRYCE	11:00A	11:00A	4:00P	DAILY		1/13	1/13	1				
21	J FAX	HEARING AID				11/27	12/17	11/27	1/12	30	8			
24	A LEE	LANDLORD				DAILY		1/12	1/12	1				

Asst. Directors W H COLEMAN-L ALLEN-H JOSLIN   Unit Prod. Manager C O ERICKSON   (WW)
F-299-C-5

Daily production report for *Rear Window*, dated January 13, 1954, the last official day of principal photography.

2 Voyeurism and the Postwar Crisis of Masculinity in *Rear Window*

Rear Window is often considered a film that thematizes cinematic spectatorship. In other words, it is considered to be a movie about watching movies.[1] L. B. Jefferies, a photojournalist for a magazine that resembles *Life,* sits transfixed for hours looking into other people's windows, just as cinema spectators gaze intently at the film screen. Indeed, the windows across the courtyard resemble miniature movie screens.[2] Because of an accident on the job, Jefferies, or Jeff as he is often called, is confined to a wheelchair much like cinematic spectators sit confined in their theater seats. A good deal of his watching occurs at night or from the shadows, just as film spectators view a film in a darkened theater. Most importantly, because Jeff seems to see his own desires and anxieties projected onto the rear windows/movie screens, the film reveals what psychoanalytic film critics have argued since the 1960s, namely that cinematic spectatorship is akin to the dream state, the state in which, according to Sigmund Freud, we symbolically fulfill our unconscious wishes.[3] Sitting immobile in the theater, isolated from the rest of the audience by virtue of the darkness, the film spectator is seemingly left alone to peer secretly at the illusion of a private world displayed on the screen. In turn, this world on the screen functions like a projected image of the spectator's own subjective fantasies.

This dynamic is at work from almost the very beginning of *Rear Window.* Just as Jeff and the camera begin to watch Lars Thorwald enter a building across the courtyard, Jeff expresses his frustration about being stuck in his apartment for six weeks. He says to his boss over the phone, "If you don't pull me out of this swamp of boredom, I'm gonna do something drastic." The camera then pans to follow Thorwald into his living room, also bringing the Thorwald's bedroom into view where Mrs. Thorwald is sitting up in bed. Eyeline matches indicate that the camera is reproducing Jeff's point of view; it looks only at what he wants to see. Jeff continues, "I'm gonna get married and then I'll never be able to go anywhere. . . . Can't you just see me rushing home to a hot apartment to listen to the automatic laundry and the electric dishwasher and the garbage disposal and a nagging wife?" As he says "nagging wife," the camera pans subjectively again to capture the Thorwalds together in their bedroom. Anna is nagging. By linking this camera movement with Jeff's comments, Hitchcock makes it clear that the viewer is watching a projection of Jeff's fears and desires. Afraid that getting married, a move he calls "drastic," would couple him with a nagging wife, Jeff chooses to look at what corroborates this fear. Later, Jeff's wish to get rid of his girlfriend, Lisa Fremont, because she is urging him to settle down with her, becomes linked to his obsession with the murder of Anna Thorwald. He watches the one rear window show out of many that best engages his unconscious fears and desires, just as film spectators see a fantasy they seem to have created, one that plays itself out as if just for them.

STELLA: We've become a race of Peeping Toms.

Discussions about the psychodynamics of cinematic spectatorship took an important turn in 1975 when Laura Mulvey published "Visual Pleasure and Narrative Cinema" in *Screen*. In the wake of the women's-rights movement of the 1960s and the introduction of feminist scholarship to academia, Mulvey used Hitchcock's 1954 film to argue for the first time in the history of film theory that gender plays a key role in the dynamics of cinematic spectatorship. Mulvey argues that Jeff's voyeurism, that which makes him representative of film spectators, is linked to his privi-

Sometimes a Telephoto Lens Is Only a Telephoto Lens: A publicity photo condenses themes of voyeurism, sexuality, and sadistic pleasure. Photo courtesy of Paramount.

lege as a man. The camera follows Jeff's look, providing the viewer with Jeff's point of view ("POV") exclusively, while Lisa, according to Mulvey, is never in a position to motivate POV shots. In other words, the camera never records her desires, either in POV shots or through other means. Rather, Mulvey argues, Lisa serves as a "passive image of visual perfection," just as all women in cinema, according to Mulvey, embody what she terms "to-be-looked-at-ness."[4] Especially once she crosses over the courtyard into Thorwald's apartment, where she thus enters the "film" Jeff is watching, Lisa becomes, as do all women, an object of the male gaze. In patriarchy, or male-dominated society, Mulvey argues, only men are in a position to see their desires projected onto the screen. Women are styled to please them.

In order to account for this situation, Mulvey turned to two premises from psychoanalysis and psychoanalytic film theory: the so-called Oedipus Complex, Freud's account of how children become gendered beings, and the kinds of pleasures generated by cinema.[5] Mulvey aimed to show that the Oedipus Complex is one of the deep, unconscious processes that the pleasure of cinema engages.

Cinema's pleasures include both the pleasure of looking and identification with an ego ideal. Following Freud, Mulvey termed the pleasure of looking "scopophilia." Literally "the love of looking," scopophilia entails subjecting people to what Mulvey terms a "controlling and curious gaze," thereby objectifying them.[6] Freud had argued that children engage in such voyeuristic activities as a means of trying to see the forbidden, especially their parents' sexual activities. Later, this drive to see becomes a component of adult sexuality. Although the images on the screen are not forbidden, the "conditions of screening and narrative conventions give the spectator an illusion of looking in on a private world," thus satisfying the urge to see and to objectify through seeing.[7]

The second way in which cinema appeals to the unconscious – identification – apparently also replicates an early stage of development in childhood. The child's ego (his or her unified sense of self) comes into being when, between six and eighteen months, the child first identifies with his or her own reflection in a mirror or with any other whole self the child perceives, say an adult. At this stage in the child's physical life, when the child is still uncoordinated, he or she mistakes the shape in the mirror with his or her own superior self. The image is thus internalized as what Freud called an "ideal ego." In short, the image of the other is narcissistically transformed into a reflection of the self in a dynamic that will be repeated throughout life in the case of all identifications. In the cinema, the human figure projected onto the screen in all of its mobility and splendor – what Mulvey terms an "idealization" or "eroticised phantasmagoria" – is experienced as an ideal ego.[8] The viewer identifies with the figure and feels enhanced and enlarged by that identification.

Because, for Mulvey, these processes are gendered, she turned to the Oedipus Complex, the supposed means by which children become gendered beings. According to Freud, the Oedipus Complex begins with the child's desire for the parent of the opposite sex and the perceived competition with the other parent that accompanies this desire. This state of affairs is interrupted when the child notes the anatomical differences between the mother and father and assumes that the mother had a penis which was subsequently cut off. The boy child gives up his incestuous desire for his mother because he fears that his father will castrate him just as, in his mind, his mother has been castrated. The boy child stops competing with his father and instead comes to identify with him, thus taking up his masculine position in society. The girl child undergoes a very different transformation. She perceives that she has already been castrated and thus, however reluctantly, identifies with her mother, thereby taking up her feminine position in society. She will henceforth be seen – and see herself – in terms of her identification with lack.

The French psychoanalyst Jacques Lacan argued subsequently that what is at stake in the Oedipus scenario is not the real penis but the phallus, the figurative representation of male power. Robin Wood's formulation in *Hitchcock's Films Revisited* of the connection between the phallus and the penis is useful here. He notes:

> Within patriarchal culture, the phallus is the supreme symbol of power; conversely, power is "phallic." Loss of power on any level (money, prestige, social status, authority over women, domination of children, etc.) is therefore symbolic castration. At the same time, this is seen as reactivating the *literal* castration fears of childhood.[9]

According to the Lacanian formulation, the Oedipus Complex, then, is the process of socialization whereby a man comes to assume patriarchal power. The woman learns through the operations of the Oedipus Complex that she lacks the phallus and consequently has no power.

Because cinema functions in patriarchal culture, the pleasures of looking at and of identifying with cinematic images are only available to those spectators who, through the Oedipus Complex, have taken their place as the dominant ones within patriarchy – that is, men. Because women lack the phallus, they have no power to shape how they will be portrayed in film and are thus portrayed in ways that the masculine gaze will find pleasurable. In short, they are made into the objects of male desire. Conversely, the men in the film will not be objectified because, Mulvey explains, "according to the principles of the ruling ideology . . . , the male figure cannot bear the burden of sexual objectification. Man is reluctant to gaze at his exhibitionist like."[10] Instead of objectifying him, spectators identify with the male protagonist. In other words, the male figure exists as the ideal ego. And it is precisely through this identification with the male figure that the spectator can possess the objectified female figure.

Mulvey argues that these pleasures and identifications, only available to men, are mobilized by them to stem the castration anxiety that arises in order to resolve the Oedipus Complex. Hence the appeal and power of cinema.

> The male unconscious has two avenues of escape from . . . castration anxiety: preoccupation with the re-enactment of the original trauma (investigating the woman, demystifying her mystery), counterbalanced by the devaluation, punishment or saving of the guilty object . . . ; or else complete disavowal of castration by the substitution of a fetish object or turning the represented figure itself into a fetish so that it becomes reassuring rather than dangerous. . . .[11]

In other words, in investigating the woman, the man can assure himself that she, not he, is castrated. Similarly, if he punishes the woman, he ensures that he is not the weak, castrated one. On the other hand, he can fetishize the woman, which is to say that he can value her glamorized figure or one of her body parts as a means of creating for himself a pleasure that overrides any danger that he might one day suffer what he imagines was her "castration." Mulvey calls these escape routes, on the one hand, "sadistic voyeurism," and, on the other, "fetishistic scopophilia." And she examines *Rear Window* as an example of the first route, arguing of Lisa and Jeff:

> When she crosses the barrier between his room and the block opposite, their relationship is reborn erotically. He does not merely watch her through his lens, as a distant meaningful image, he also sees her as a guilty intruder exposed by a dangerous man threatening her with punishment, and thus finally giving him the opportunity to save her.[12]

In short, by viewing her as a guilty object, namely because she is a trespasser, Jeff takes the first avenue of defense against castration anxiety – sadistic voyeurism – and, by virtue of their identification with Jeff, so too do the film's spectators. Within Mulvey's schema, female viewers must also objectify Lisa and therefore themselves.

In the wake of this argument, many questioned Mulvey's assertion that women can only objectify themselves when watching cinema or, in other words, can only be masochistic spectators.[13] One feminist film critic questioned this premise by also turning to *Rear Window*. In her 1988 book, *The Women Who Knew Too Much: Hitchcock and Feminist Theory*, Tania Modleski joined many other feminist critics of the 1970s and 1980s who argued that women are inherently different from men, but not because in supposedly lacking the phallus they are less powerful. Rather, Modleski and other "difference" feminists submitted that women might be powerful in their own right and in different ways than men. Whereas Mulvey argues that men are afraid of castration because they are afraid that it will make them woman-like, namely weak, Modleski argues that men are afraid that women aren't castrated at all. Men are afraid that women "may not, after all, be mutilated (imperfect) men, may not be what as . . . [one critic] puts it *men* would be if they lacked penises – 'bereft of sexuality, helpless, incapable.'"[14]

Based on this supposed inherent difference between men and women, Modleski argues that the two are very different kinds of cinematic spectators. She asserts that, because *Rear Window* represents not only Jeff's point of view but also Lisa's in the many reaction shots that contain both of them within the frame, the film has much to tell us about the differences between how Jeff, a man, and Lisa, a woman, spectate.[15] She finds that, whereas a man objectifies the female figure on the screen, as Mulvey argues, a woman spectator identifies and empathizes with that figure.[16] By way of an example, Modleski considers that Jeff sees Miss Torso as "a queen bee with her pick of the drones," whereas Lisa, by comparing Miss Torso's apartment to her own, sees that Miss Torso is "doing a woman's hardest job – juggling wolves," an interpretation that, Modleski notes, proves correct at the film's end when Stanley, Miss Torso's true love, arrives – to her obvious delight. Through their own identificatory and empathetic means of spectating, female viewers of the film, according to Modleski, will not masochistically objectify Lisa or themselves but will see that Lisa's desire to marry Jeff leads her into the clutches of a wife murderer. And thus where Mulvey sees Hitchcock as representative of Hollywood patriarchal cinema, Modleski sees him as working outside of it, as evidenced, according to her, by his ambivalence about women. Female spectators of *Rear Window* must endure the murder of a wife but are also empowered in their recognition that Lisa's seemingly normal desires for a husband endanger her.

Both Mulvey's and Modleski's arguments have much to teach us, not only about cinematic spectatorship within patriarchy, but also about *Rear Window* in particular. One thing feminist psychoanalytic film criticism (Mulvey) and "difference" feminism (Modleski) haven't been able to provide adequately, however, is an attentiveness to the historical specificity of gender dynamics. Patriarchy, and patriarchal cinema for that matter, have functioned differently at different times. In *Rear Window,* for example, when Jeff whines that if he doesn't get out of his apartment soon he'll do something "drastic," he equates marriage not only with a "nagging wife" but with "rushing home to a hot apartment to listen to the automatic laundry and the electric dishwasher and the garbage disposal." It is true that his apartment is now hot and might be as hot in the future, as evidenced by a shot of his thermometer reading ninety-three degrees at the opening of the film.

If the Gaze Is Male, What Is the Reaction Shot?: Lisa and Jeff share a reaction shot. Photo courtesy of Paramount.

And Anna Thorwald's behavior makes the point that wives can be nags. But nowhere in the film is there any evidence that, through marriage, Jeff will own or even encounter a washing machine, dishwasher, or garbage disposal. So why does he evoke them here, much less connect them to a nagging wife? This is a question that, like many others raised by the film, requires a look at the specific conditions and dynamics of fifties culture in the United States.

JEFF: Can you see me driving down to the fashion salon in a jeep, wearing combat boots and a three-day beard?

The years following World War II (1941–45) resulted in a new place in America: suburbia. An economic boom fueled by defense spending during and after the war made it possible for many to fulfill the desire to escape urban problems and to get more house for the money. In 1954, the year that *Rear Window* was released, 1.5 million new homes were built, most of them in the suburbs. By then, 20 percent of the population lived there. For Thomas

Hine, author of *Populux,* an account of American life in the fifties and sixties, the fact that even TV's Lucy and Ricky Ricardo moved from their apartment in Manhattan to a house in Westport, Connecticut, demonstrates that "the most successful institution had to make the move to suburbia to maintain credibility with the audience."[17]

The now more isolated family units that composed the suburbs were typically managed by women. During the war, women had moved into the workplace to fill the shoes of the absent men and to fill their own empty purses. Eager to have the soldiers reassert their masculine roles at home after the war, American culture immediately began to idolize those women who returned home to be wives and mothers. In other words, June Cleaver quickly replaced Rosie the Riveter as the ideal American woman. The economic boom resulted in an array of domestic appliances meant to assist women in their new role. Hine explains, "[A]ppliance manufacturers . . . during the early 1950s . . . brought out a parade of new products they hoped would be mainstays of the new suburban households. Some, like the automatic clothes washer, and later the dryer, took hold right away."[18] *Rear Window* is of an age when consumers were being bombarded with the message that such appliances, aimed as they were specifically at stay-at-home mothers, were somehow connected to a familial bliss supposedly available only in the suburbs.

But if one of the ideals of fifties America was a house in suburbia full of time-saving gadgets run by a cheerful lady of the house, Jeff imagines the exact opposite of that particular ideal. In his mind, marriage will yoke him, not to a suburban wife grateful for automated aid, but to one who, like Anna Thorwald, makes her husband's life as miserable emotionally as a hot apartment in the city does physically. There is something about the new ideal in which Jeff can't believe or that he doesn't feel will accrue to him.

The war had allowed men to prove that they were the nation's protectors. After the war, however, the new responsibilities at home and in the workplace didn't make men feel as masculine as the risk and adventure they had experienced overseas once had.[19]

Nor were there the means once available to assuage previous crises in masculinity. In the late nineteenth century, for example, Theodore Roosevelt and others turned to the rugged outdoors as a means of rejuvenating men seemingly emasculated by modernity. The frontier became, in essence, a giant theme park.[20] In two speeches, "The Strenuous Life" (1899) and "The Pioneer Spirit and American Problems" (1900), Roosevelt railed against "the cloistered life which saps the hardy virtues." He called for men to follow the "strenuous life."[21] Aiming to make such a life available to people, Roosevelt created five national parks and fifty-one wildlife refuges and founded both the Rough Riders and the Boone and Crockett Club. According to Michael Kimmel, author of *Manhood in America: A Cultural History*, "testing manhood . . . [became] increasingly difficult," however, by the early twentieth century. "The public arena was crowded and competitive, and heading west to start over was more the stuff of fiction than possibility" (157). In the wake of this particular crisis of masculinity, Westerns became increasingly popular as a way for men to live in fantasy what they felt unable to live in reality. By the fifties, John Wayne consistently topped popularity polls as the figure most admired by American men.

Jeff is a returning soldier himself, as detective Tom Doyle's repartee with him reminds us. ("How did we ever stand each other in that plane for three years during the war?") Against the suburban ideal himself, Jeff is eager to shun what Roosevelt called "the cloistered life" in favor of the exotic frontiers to which his postwar job takes him. At various points throughout the film, Shanghai, Brazil, Hong Kong, and the Himalayas are evoked as his possible destinations. Jeff wants to conceive of himself as a man in the Roosevelt/Wayne tradition, as evidenced in particular by his description of his job, whereby he tries to convince Lisa that she isn't "cut out" for his kind of life:

> Did you ever eat fish heads and rice? . . . Did you ever try to keep warm in a C-54 at 15,000 feet, twenty degrees below zero? . . . Did you ever get shot at? Did you ever get run over? Did you ever get sandbagged at night because somebody got unfavorable publicity

from your camera? . . . Lisa, in this job you carry one suitcase. Your
home is the available transportation. You don't sleep very much.
You bathe less. And sometimes the food that you eat is made from
things that you couldn't even look at when they're alive!

Lisa wants him to give up traveling, preferring him to work in
the city in a "dark blue flannel suit" so that they can have a future
together, by which we must surmise that she wants to marry him.
(Her glee at finding Anna Thorwald's wedding ring, which she
flashes triumphantly at Jeff, serves as evidence of this.) But even as
she imagines that he will look "handsome" in such an outfit, for
others the business suit was a symbol of conformity. Books as
diverse as *The Man in the Grey Flannel Suit* (1955), a novel, and
Must We Conform? (1955), a psychological study, indicate that
many middle-class men of the fifties felt emasculated by conformity. It's not surprising, then, that Jeff strives to have a very different image of himself: "Can you see me driving down to the fashion salon in a jeep, wearing combat boots and a three-day beard?"
But because the fulfillment of his masculine fantasies isn't available to him, as it wasn't for so many men of the post–World War
II period, Jeff is feminized. Stuck at home, he has become a version of the stay-at-home wife himself. His broken leg serves as a
symbol of his figurative castration.

By having Jeff stuck at home where he thus has a feminized
position and Lisa, conversely, spending her days at work, Hitchcock reverses the stereotypical gender roles for the period. Jeff is
the one who feels so trapped by his confinement that he is ready
to do something "drastic," whereas Lisa is the one who comes into
the domestic sphere only after an exciting day at work (at least
until late in the film when she has become intrigued by the "rear
window" show, and yet even her one daytime appearance is on a
Saturday if we consider that the film starts on a Wednesday). Also
manlike for the fifties is the fact that Lisa never cooks a meal;
instead, she uses take-out (albeit from an exclusive restaurant). Jeff
lashes out at Lisa on various occasions for reasons that seem linked
to their role reversal. After asking about her day, he follows up with

a question about what one of the women at a meeting was wearing – a question a wife might ask. When Lisa proceeds to tell him, he interrupts her with teasing sarcasm in order to make his disdain for such details evident. Later that evening, when Lisa attempts to convince him that she, too, could travel to even the most remote places, he becomes sadistic, barking at her to "Shut up!"

Lisa's role as a working woman was not an aberrant one, however. For it was not the case that the new ideal of the stay-at-home wife succeeded in driving all women out of the workplace. Historian James T. Patterson, author of *Grand Expectations: The United States, 1945–1974*, explains that, after the war, "demobilization drove many of these women from . . . [their] jobs, but it only briefly slowed what was already a powerful long-range trend toward greater female participation in the market." Women were working more and needing the fulfillment of work outside of the home. "The majority gradually came to need both, at least for stretches of their lives, and encountered all the satisfactions and tribulations of juggling the two." By 1950, there were 18 million women working for pay, only a million or so fewer than in 1945. Patterson expresses a view now common among historians when he asserts that "the rise in female employment was one of the most powerful demographic trends of the postwar era."[22]

Lisa not only fits into this demographic trend but relishes her career. Although Jeff insists to Stella that Lisa only cares about "a new dress, and a lobster dinner, and the latest scandal," the film shows her manifesting a deep concern about many facets of the business within which she works: fashion. She is concerned about whether clothes will sell or not, asking Jeff of the $1,100 dress she models for him when we are first introduced to her, "Do you think it'll sell?" In his response, Jeff's sarcasm seems to stem from the fact that he is imitating calculations he may have heard her do before: "That depends on the quote, you know. Let's see now. There's the plane ticket over, and import duties, hidden taxes, profit markup." Lisa explains that "we" sell a dozen in this price range. "Even if I had to pay, it would be worth it – just for the occasion." The dress seems to have been complimentary or on loan to her. Many critics have thus assumed that Lisa is a model.[23] But this is impossible if we consider that her description of her day indicates that whatever job she has involves her in the business decisions of an entity of which she considers herself an integral part. Her use of "we" associates her further with a proprietary rather than employee role:

> I was all morning in a sales meeting. Then I had to dash to the Waldorf for a quick drink with Madame Dufrene, who is just over from Paris with some spy reports. And then I had to go to "21" to have lunch with the *Harper's Bazaar* people – and that's when I ordered dinner. Then I had two Fall showings twenty blocks apart. Then I had to have a cocktail with Leland and Slim Hayward – we're trying to get his new show. Then I had to dash back and change.

Leland Hayward was a stage producer and talent agent. As an agent, Hayward actually bought, then sold to Hitchcock the Woolrich story on which *Rear Window* was based. The reference to him in the film is thus an inside joke. (See the chapter by Scott Curtis in this volume.) (His wife, nicknamed "Slim," had previously been married to film director Howard Hawks.) It would be highly unlikely that a model of the fifties, no matter what her social connections, would be trotted out to meet so many important people, especially to either gather "secrets," make a deal with "the . . . people" from an important fashion magazine, or to contract with a producer for his next show. That her job is an important one is further corroborated by the fact that she makes good money. She pays for a lobster dinner for two from the very expensive "21" where she seems to be a frequent patron – she is on a first-name basis with Carl, the waiter – and for Carl's tip and taxi fare home. We are told, too, that she lives in "the high rent district."

That Hitchcock specifically meant Lisa to be a business woman, in addition to being a model, is evidenced by a 1974 deposition in which he testified in court that he patterned Lisa on Anita Colby (1914–1992).[24] Indeed, the similarities between the beautiful blond and the Lisa character as played by Grace Kelly are such that audi-

America's No. 1 Cover Girl, Anita Colby, models the latest fashions against a bamboo-curtained background. "The 'Face' has a brain to match." Photo courtesy of Paramount.

ence members might have recognized parallels beyond just the one of similar looks. Colby was what modeling expert Michael Gross deems the world's first supermodel.[25] At the height of her modeling career, she appeared on fifteen magazine covers in one month. Soon thereafter, in 1938, she astonished everyone by taking a job at *Harper's Bazaar* as an ad salesperson. Her savvy reasoning: "A model's days are numbered."[26] Colby became a top money earner at *Harper's Bazaar* even as she kept modeling for greater and greater fees. Like Colby, the Lisa character works with people from *Harper's*. And Hitchcock closes the film with her studying this flagship of the fashion magazines.

After *Harper's,* Colby moved on to a business career in Holly-
wood. In 1945, while the "Feminine Director" of David O.
Selznick's studio, Colby's picture was splashed on the cover of
Time magazine over the headline: "HOLLYWOOD'S ANITA COLBY: 'The
Face' has a brain to match" (January 8, 1945). According to the
Time article, her job at Selznick's studio

> combine[d] . . . the talents of ace trouble shooter, talent scout,
> fashion expert, beauty expert and housemother. Ingrid Bergman
> would prefer not to be photographed unless Colby is on hand.
> Jennifer Jones thinks twice about blowing her nose without
> reporting to Colby. Independent of Publicity Chief Don King, she
> works closely with Selznick, handling all deals public and per-
> sonal which call for grade-A finesse. Her social and journalistic
> contacts in both New York and Hollywood are peerless. . . . To all
> the people on earth who most matter to David Selznick, she is an
> indispensable one-woman pipeline.[27]

Indeed, her days were so hectic that, according to *Time,* she had to
be hospitalized at one point for exhaustion. Hitchcock's Lisa also
reports whirlwind days in the business world where she, too,
seems the center of numerous projects.

Colby was also well known for an equally full social life meant
specifically to fuel her business success. *Time* reported that "each
evening, until a normal 3 a.m., she keeps right on working – at
parties. . . . It is not extraordinary for Colby to go to three parties
in an evening." The article makes a point of noting that it was her
nightly presence at the Stork Club in New York City that had led
to Colby's "discovery." In a recent interview, Colby's sister,
Francine Counihan, substantiates that a family friend brought the
two sisters to all the big parties in New York City so that they
could become well connected. Counihan recalls, "It was 'Twenty-
one' [sic], Stork Club, El Morocco, tea dancing at the Plaza
Hotel."[28] Of course, this is the same "21" where Lisa has a business
lunch and where she is such a regular that she knows the waiter
by name. Such clubs and restaurants were known to be the haunts
of movers and shakers.

Colby was still very much on the public scene in the early years of the fifties. In 1952, Prentice-Hall published *Anita Colby's Beauty Book* with simultaneous publication in London. The book was successful enough to warrant reprinting in 1953. In 1953 and 1954, the years during which Hitchcock was making and releasing *Rear Window,* Colby was the TV Hostess of the Pepsi-Cola Playhouse. And she was still a glamorous object of the Hollywood rumor mill where it was reported that she had earlier turned down marriage offers from Clark Gable and James Stewart, Hitchcock's leading man.[29] (She didn't marry until she was fifty-six.) Colby's supposed romantic connection to Stewart, her modeling, and her business drive are combined by Hitchcock in the character of Lisa: part beautiful romance object, part model strutting her lavish wardrobe on the catwalk of Jeff's apartment, part zealous businesswoman. And fifties audiences would have had practice finding this combination plausible in the well-known person of Anita Colby.

Given Lisa's vivacity and her devotion to Jeff, not to mention the beauty Grace Kelly brings to the part, it is incomprehensible to Stella and even to us that Jeff doesn't want to marry Lisa. In the early fifties, young men who didn't want to marry and who remained single for too long were considered "emotionally immature" or "latent homosexuals," phrases that Arlene Skolnick, the author of *Embattled Paradise: The American Family in an Age of Uncertainty,* says were "part of the basic vocabulary of the 1950s."[30] So when Jeff says petulantly that he doesn't want to marry Lisa, Stella brands that "abnormal." Stella hints again at the possibility that Jeff is abnormal or perverse when she queries: "Is what you want something you can discuss?" Even Lisa worries at one point that Jeff has problems when he fails to respond to her physical advances. (Jeff: "What do you think?" Lisa: "Something too frightful to utter.") And certainly the film's narrative implies that Jeff is perverse insofar as the only sexual activity he desires and seeks to satisfy is voyeurism.

And yet it was also the case that, in 1954, the year Hitchcock released *Rear Window,* a new day was dawning for single men in America. A new magazine had just debuted in December 1953 that advocated an ideal whereby a man enjoyed women's company but shunned the constraint of marriage. An early issue of Hugh Heffner's *Playboy* proclaimed:

> Take a good look at the sorry, regimented husbands trudging down every woman-dominated street in this woman-dominated land. . . . Don't bother asking their advice. Almost to a man, they'll tell you marriage is the greatest. *Naturally.* Do you expect them to admit they made the biggest mistake of their lives?[31]

The magazine's coup was that it created a means of avoiding the then-standard charge that men who remained single must be homosexual or otherwise perverse. Barbara Ehrenreich remarks in her book, *The Hearts of Men: American Dreams and the Flight from Commitment,* that "when the articles railed against the responsibilities of marriage, there were the nude torsos to reassure you that the alternative was still within the bounds of heterosexuality."[32] In short, *Playboy's* debut in 1953 marks the first time that there was an attempt to give single men status. When Jeff says to Stella that he'll "probably get married one of these days," we know that, in the meantime, he will continue to enjoy looking at Miss Torso and other scantily clad women. Recall that, after taking his temperature one morning, Stella declares that he's got a "hormone deficiency" because "those bathing beauties you've been watching haven't raised your temperature one degree in a month." The joke here, of course, is that Jeff has spent an inordinate amount of time staring intently out of his window at these "bathing beauties." It must be the case, then, that, inspite of what Stella concludes, they do raise his so-called temperature. So it certainly isn't the case that Jeff lacks the requisite heterosexual desire. As he informs Lisa later, he wants his relationship with her to remain "status quo." In other words, he wants what physical and emotional intimacy they share without the marriage commitment. Like *Playboy,* when Jeff does think of marriage, he can conjure up only the opposite of the fifties marriage ideal.

But it is also the case that Jeff has reasons for not wanting to marry Lisa in particular. Relying on Jeff's own assertion, Modleski argues that he is afraid of Lisa's perfection. But his fear of marriage to her seems linked to her sexual assertiveness. Hitchcock first introduces Lisa to us while she is greeting Jeff with a long, sensuous kiss. The director portrays her assertiveness here as dangerous or at least intimidating to Jeff. He captures the kiss in three consecutive shots: first as a shadow cast across Jeff's face, then as a looming close-up from Jeff's point of view, and finally as a stepped-camera shot of the kiss itself.[33] That evening, when Lisa shifts her position within the frame while making her case that she and Jeff should be together, the Newlyweds' window comes into view. Hitchcock thus underscores that the kind of assertiveness manifested in Lisa's proposition is motivated by the same sexual desire seen earlier through their window. He introduces the pair the next evening with a medium close-up shot of Lisa on Jeff's lap. She is very intent on enjoying this physical moment. Noting that Jeff's mind is elsewhere, she asserts, "I want all of you." Rather than responding eagerly, as Stella would have him do, Jefferies asks, "Don't you ever have any problems?" She replies, "I have one now," referring to his obvious lack of interest. According to him, however, his problem is that he can't figure out "why a man [would] leave his apartment three times on a rainy night with a suitcase and come back three times." Lisa can only interpret Jeff's question through the lens of love and sexuality, replying that he "likes the way his wife welcomes him home." We might say that, when faced with Lisa and her desires, Jeff can't get it up, as the expression goes. Robbing him of his potency with her assertiveness, Lisa makes him even more feminized than he already is. Jeff's explanation that his problem with Lisa is that she is "too perfect" and too interested in fashion, gossip, and her rich lifestyle is undermined; he doesn't want her because she unmans him.

Lisa's sexual assertiveness may have been surprising for viewers who didn't expect as much from the cool, socialite Grace Kelly.[34] And yet that women had strong sexual appetites was an idea being widely discussed in the early fifties.[35] Alfred Kinsey, founder and brainchild of the Institute for Sex Research of Indiana University, had just followed up his 1948 best-selling and controversial study, *Sexual Behavior in the Human Male,* with *Sexual Behavior in the Human Female.* Published in 1953, this study, like his first, was based on the findings of hundreds of sexual histories he and his students had taken in the 1940s. Despite being 842 pages long, the book became a best seller. Among other things, he stated that nearly 50 percent of females had premarital sex, that many women masturbated, and that many more women had extramarital affairs than the general public wanted to believe. His statistics scared and infuriated many. In 1954, for example, the Rockefeller Foundation cut off his funding. So, too, in *Rear Window,* are there those who see women's sexuality as aberrant. Doyle looks suspiciously at Lisa's overnight case, viewing her behavior as a violation of what he seems to consider proper female behavior. (This is not to say that Doyle himself never strays; Jeff has to remind Doyle of his wife when he becomes transfixed by Miss Torso.) When Jeff argues that Thorwald didn't tell his landlord that his wife was leaving for good because "he was hiding something," Doyle looks at the bag and asks Jeff if he tells *his* landlord everything, again showing his suspicion of Lisa's behavior. Despite the fact that her assertive sexuality might have been seen as perfectly normal, especially given Kinsey's findings, Lisa's sexual assertiveness makes Doyle wary and intimidates Jeff.

This seems to be because the film links Lisa's sexual assertiveness specifically to her professional identity in the public sphere, the sphere from which Jeff's accident has barred him. Her attempts to seduce him always occur after the workday, when she reenters the domestic realm to which women "properly" belong. And she uses the outfits of her profession in her attempts to create an image appealing enough to seduce Jeff. Finally, the fact that they have reversed the public/private gender roles of the fifties is what allows her to come to his house to initiate an overnight stay. Scholar Elaine Tyler May concurs of the period in general that "society saw that the increasing expression of female sexuality and women's entering the paid labor force were two sides of the same dangerous coin."[36] In both cases, women were entering the world of men or at least emulating male behaviors. If Jeff doesn't want to marry Lisa, it is because her job keeps her in the public sphere, the sphere in which he rightfully belongs but from which he has been banned. His fear of her sexuality could certainly be a symptom of this larger issue.

LISA: I'll trade you my feminine intuition for a bed for the night.
JEFF: I'll go along with that.

Because he is afraid of Lisa's assertiveness and frustrated with his feminization, Jeff denigrates women's knowledge, perhaps as a means of protecting himself from further feminization. When Stella admonishes Jeff for spying and suggests that people ought to look into their own houses, he dismisses what she calls a "bit of home-spun philosophy" by sarcastically asserting that she got it from the April 1939 edition of *Reader's Digest,* a popular magazine and yet one that, as a compilation magazine, never has a thought of its own. By implication, Stella and other proponents of the "home-spun," usually women, don't either. Next, when she insists that she predicted the stock market crash of 1929 by noting how many times a GM executive had to urinate, Jeff dismisses her observation as irrational, presumably a feminine trait, insisting that "in economics, a kidney ailment has no relation to the stock market, none whatsoever."

Jeff's attempts to solve Anna Thorwald's disappearance soon transform him, however, into a great proponent of women's ways of knowing when what both Lisa and Doyle call "feminine intuition" makes plausible his hunch that Anna was murdered. Ultimately, Jeff champions this way of knowing even when Doyle, a war buddy and thus one of Jeff's means of access to masculine identification, disdains it. Jeff's transformation first occurs when Lisa presents a theory about the wife's jewelry. On a previous night, when Lisa turned on the apartment's three lights and paused briefly at each to pose in her $1,100 dress, she wasn't successful in capturing Jeff's desire. This time, when she repeats her circle around the room, she accompanies the action with speculations about the murder and, as a result, is effective in capturing his attention. When she explains to Jeff about women's handbags, he is riveted by her for the first time, twisting away from the window awkwardly in order to keep her in his sight even as she pauses periodically to look out the window, typically *his* preferred pastime. "Why, a woman going anywhere but the hospital would always take makeup, perfume, and jewelry!" She helps Jeff put away his camera and zoom lens, a sign that they can now rely on *her* powers of perception, as centered around the handbag theory for which she uses her own bag as a demonstration. More specifically, the scene enacts a switch from male equipment for looking (camera as phallus) to female equipment for being looked at (purses carry make-up and jewelry).[37] He asks, "That's inside stuff, huh?" And when she replies that "it's basic equipment," he concurs, "Well, I'm with you sweetie. I'm with you." This marks the first time that he values women's ways of knowing.

By the time Doyle joins them, Jeff firmly positions himself on the side of women's ways of knowing, even as Doyle denigrates women. When Lisa asserts that the handbag can only lead to one conclusion, Jeff even finishes her thought: "It was not Mrs. Thorwald that left yesterday morning." After listening for a while to their speculations, Doyle interrupts with biting sarcasm even as he echoes Lisa's term for her particular expertise: "Look, Miss Fremont, that feminine intuition stuff sells magazines but, in real life, it's still a fairy tale. I don't know how many wasted years I've spent tracking down leads based on female intuition." Jeff takes it upon himself to drain this critique of any legitimacy, thus for the first time also defending Lisa's career. After all, part of her career is to help sell magazines such as *Harper's Bazaar*. "All right . . . all this is from an old speech you once made at the Policeman's Ball." Interestingly, here Jeff refers to an event whose purpose is ostensibly for the legal profession to dance with women even as Doyle's speech at the ball serves as an opportunity to show how incompetent women are at upholding the law. In short, Jeff exposes the ideological underpinnings of Doyle's remark and, by extension, fifties gender politics: Men want women to stand by them socially but not professionally.

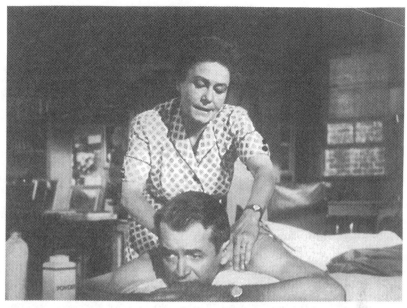

Reader's Digest, 1939: Jeff dismisses women's ways of knowing. Photo courtesy of Paramount.

Right after Lisa offers him her theory, Jeff makes his first sexual overture, pulling Lisa onto his lap. When she matches this overture, proposing, "I'll trade you my feminine intuition for a bed for the night," Jeff says he'll "go along with that." He is finally interested in her sexual assertiveness after she has offered him information about women that will help him solve the murder case. In other words, it is this newfound interest in women's way of knowing that transforms Jeff into an active heterosexual male, not merely a sexual voyeur. He starts the scene "diseased," Lisa's term for his spying and a term that resonates with Stella's warning that he is "abnormal." Toward the end of the scene, however, he is on the road to a cure. And so the curtains come down on the rear window show for the first time since Hitchcock opened them at the onset of the film. And, significantly, it is Lisa who draws them, noting, "Show's over for tonight." She terms the diaphanous nightgown and matching slippers spilling out of her handbag a "preview of coming attractions." In short, with one show seemingly over, Jeff is ready to begin another one that entails sharing a bed with a woman who reenters the scene bedecked in lingerie. Not until Jeff has accepted women's ways of knowing and thus their careers does his fear of their supposed sexual assertiveness diminish.

LISA: Jeff, if you're squeamish, just don't look.

Modleski is right to note that the film contains other point-of-view shots besides those motivated by Jefferies. What she fails to note, however, is that there is a shift in the film from Jeff's point of view to point-of-view shots from both Lisa and Stella, a shift related directly to the film's increased privileging of women's ways of knowing. After opening with an omniscient crane and pan that reads both the courtyard and Jeff's apartment, the film oscillates between omniscient shots and Jeff's POV, the latter enabled first by binoculars and then by a telephoto lens. At a certain point, however, the film begins to include POV shots from the two women. When Jeff takes out the slides he took of the garden, we look at the slides first from Lisa's and then from Stella's point of view. It is true, of course, that Jeff created these images and that he has to teach the two women how to look at them. Nevertheless, the film assumes a continuity between the two women and the audience, seemingly comfortable in thus feminizing the latter. Later, it is Stella who, borrowing what she refers to as Jeff's "portable keyhole," correctly reads Miss Lonely Hearts's situation as suicidal. Her reading is not dependent on her empathy nor on any identification, as Modleski would have it, but rather on her knowledge as a professional nurse. Based on the color of the pills Miss Lonely Hearts lays out, Stella is able to tell that they are rodium tri-eckonal. Once Stella and Lisa have gone to investigate, at Stella's suggestion, Jeff looks again at Miss Lonely Hearts and decides that Stella was wrong, perhaps signaling his continued resistance to her way of looking. When Stella returns to his apartment and resumes looking with him, however, we get another shot of Miss Lonely Hearts from Stella's point of view that proves

Stella right and, having to concur this time, Jeff calls the police. This becomes a fortunate circumstance because Jeff is already on the line with them when Thorwald returns and can immediately enlist their aid. (Of course, on the other hand, if Stella hadn't directed Jeff's attention to Miss Lonely Hearts and thus away from Lisa, then Jeff would have been able to call her when Thorwald approached, giving her time to get out, as Lisa had requested.)

Lisa and Stella's increased control of the camera's look seems linked to their increasingly active role in the case. Jeff even remarks on this when Lisa and Stella plot to dig in the garden. Noting that they can scare Thorwald again, he pauses, "But I guess I'm using 'we' too freely. You're taking all the risk." Lisa responds in the vein of an exclusive club, in this case a *women's* club: "Shall we vote him in, Stella?" Stella responds, "Unanimously." This contrasts sharply with Lisa's initial attempt to gather evidence when she referred to it as her "assignment," presumably making Jefferies the boss and taking on the role for herself of his "Girl Friday." Now she and Stella not only are living the kind of life Jeff wants his wife to lead – "I want a woman who will go anywhere and do anything and love it" – but they are also in charge of that life.

As Lisa and Stella gain control of the investigation and of the camera's look, Jeff loses control and can no longer look.[38] When Stella and Lisa plot to dig up whatever is in the garden and Jeff protests, Lisa advises, "Jeff, if you're squeamish, just don't look." Jeff protests: "Squeamish! I'm not squeamish! I just don't want you two to end up like that dog ended up. That's all." But while his concern may indeed be motivated by his feelings for the women, it is very true that he *is* squeamish and the film has made a point of conveying this. Earlier, when Stella speculated about how Thorwald killed his wife, Jeff was unable to eat the meal she had served him despite having just exclaimed over it that it was no wonder that her husband still loved her. Conversely, Stella munches on a piece of toast throughout her gory speculations. By assuming that Jeff will need to look away, Lisa assumes a staunchness on her own part and on that of Stella that she can't imagine Jeff shares. Then, when Lisa is being roughed up by Thorwald, Jeff cringes, forcing himself to watch when he can hardly bear it. (This echoes the earlier assault scene when Miss Lonely Hearts was being assaulted by a man she met at the bar across the street. Lisa watched unflinchingly while Jeff looked away.) And when Jeff pops off four flashbulbs in an attempt to stall the approaching Thorwald, he has to look away from each flash in order to avoid being blinded himself. Hitchcock makes a point of showing Jeff looking away and covering his eyes each time. Finally, the film ends with Jeff's eyes completely closed, as they were at the opening of the film, allowing Lisa to read *Harper's Bazaar* rather than a travel book, *Beyond the High Himalayas*.[39] If Hitchcock doesn't give us Lisa's POV in the final scene, that may be because he has brought us back to the same omniscient camera crane and pan that opened the film. Nevertheless, it is Lisa who is shown looking, fixing the sleeping Jeff in her gaze. We might even say that, with his second broken leg, Jeff has been punished for looking whereas Lisa has not, another major reversal of typical fifties gender dynamics. (Consider, for example, *Kiss Me Deadly* [1955], in which, despite being warned of Lot's wife, the femme fatale is turned to ashes for trying to look inside a box of nuclear material the film equates with Pandora's box.)

That their respective transformations – Jeff into a user and advocate of women's knowledge and Lisa into a person who can motivate the camera's look – are related is most clearly evidenced by the fact that Lisa's first POV shot in the film occurs during the same scene in which Jeff is transformed. The camera follows her look at the Song Writer's apartment when "that song," as she calls the piece in progress, starts again. She wonders, "Where does a man get inspiration to write a song like that?" Lying down on the settee, Lisa notes that "it's utterly beautiful. I wish I could be creative." Lisa's position on the settee and within the frame is such that, during these remarks immediately following her first POV, she and Jeff form an "X" or cross. The cross is a literal embodiment in the mise-en-scène of the switch enacted in this scene from Jeff's belittling to championing what the film calls "feminine

The Switch: Lisa's status begins to shift from that of spectacle to that of active participant in the investigation. Photo courtesy of Paramount.

intuition" and Lisa's going from spectacle working hard to be looked at to active participant in the murder investigation.

And yet the question is a funny one for Lisa to be asking. Jeff imagines that her creativity is solely sexual. He responds, "Oh, sweetie you are. You have a great talent for creating difficult situations . . . staying here all night, uninvited." That she is sexually creative not only has been proved by her various means of attempting to attract Jeff, but seems to be echoed in her reclining position on the settee. Indeed, her wish hardly seems motivated by anything we know about her. Professionally, she has also shown herself to be extremely creative. She wears the clothes "expected" of her, as she says, and knows the people who can help her and her company ("we") attain success. Hitchcock's attempt here to make her disown any creativity thus rings false in this scene and throughout the rest of the film, where it has been through Lisa's creativity and initiation of ideas and actions that the murder is solved. So why does Hitchcock make her say this line?

Importantly, Lisa's POV shot here is an echo of Hitchcock's gaze for he, too, during his cameo, looked at the Song Writer. The echo reveals Hitchcock's own wish to identify with a woman whose knowledge and creativity make her very powerful. His film fulfills that wish by celebrating "feminine intuition," even as Hitchcock, like Jeff, attempts to contain women's power by either sexualizing it or making them disown it. Lisa's wish for creativity, coming as it does at a moment that echoes Hitchcock's own gaze, seems an attempt by the director to undermine or soften the power to which Jeff and he will ascribe – a power that, in the film, belongs specifically to women.

So to the extent that Lisa is what Mulvey terms an "image," she is not a passive one but rather a self-made and self-directed image, an image "loaded to her fingertips," as Stella says, not only with love for Jeff but with her own agency. Lisa learns quickly that in order to grab Jeff's attention, she is going to have to compete with the rear window spectacle. Even when Jeff asserts that he will no longer spy on his neighbors and instead rehearse the old precept "to love thy neighbor," she has to compete with Miss Torso. So she draws the shades, responding to the interest he voices in the Torso peep show: "Not if I have to move into an apartment across the way and do the dance of the seven veils every hour." When she begins the new "show," she enters wearing her nightgown like a model walking on a fashion show runway, striking poses that alternate with twirls. She is not the "passive image" here Mulvey imagines but, rather, purposefully makes herself a show. When her attempt to make herself a spectacle is interrupted by the scream that signals the murder of the dog that "knew too much," she then takes another tack, going across the courtyard to join the spectacle with which Jeff is obsessed. And while it is true that Jeff starts to pay attention to Lisa earlier, once she becomes involved in his speculations about a murder, it is her return from delivering the letter to Thorwald that sparks his most loving gaze at her yet.

Once Lisa has been arrested, Jeff tries frantically to get the bail money together for Lisa right away, despite the fact that she can't possibly have even arrived at the police station yet. In his new-found love for Lisa, he seems to be afraid to let other men near her. Stella reminds him that he has cause to worry: "When the Cops see Lisa, they'll give *me* two hundred and fifty dollars." Whatever the case, Jeff has only $127, prompting Stella to search in Lisa's purse. Whereas earlier in the film purses meant women's sexuality (Lisa's nightgown and slippers), the clue to a murder (Anna Thorwald's wedding ring), and, through the purse with the nightgown that Lisa uses to demonstrate Anna Thorwald's situation, finally both (female sexuality as criminal), here Lisa's purse contains only fifty cents. This seems surprising considering that in an earlier scene she had enough money to pay for an entire dinner for two from "21" plus the waiter's tip and cab fare! Having carried so much significance throughout the film, purses come up virtually empty. The difference seems to be who is looking in the purses. When men look in women's purses, they find things that they can load with significance, in this case with sexuality and guilt. When women look in women's purses, however, the purses come up empty. *Rear Window* thus reveals that the significance given purses by men has more to do with the men than with the purses or the women who own them. Also notable in this scene is the fact that, after Stella looks in Lisa's purse, Jeff hands his tele-photo lens over to her, echoing the earlier scene in which he gave it to Lisa to put away. It seems that because he is once again using a woman as his surrogate and co-conspirator – this time sending Stella to the police station – he has to give up his phallic power. Hitchcock's film doesn't reiterate fifties gender ideals and dynamics but exposes them for what they are, even offering a way out.

Preoccupied with the bail money, both Jeff and Stella fail to see Thorwald leave his apartment. Film theorist Jeanne Allen makes the point that Lisa is responsible for the fact that Thorwald is both directed to and left free to confront Jeff once the police arrive at Thorwald's apartment. She notes that Lisa could have accused Thorwald in front of the police, a point that Thorwald himself understands. He asks Jeff, "What do you want from me? Your friend, the girl, could have turned me in. Why didn't she?" Allen writes of this:

> Thorwald *assumes* Jefferies is the director, but this has been Lisa's decision. *What did she want?* To have him take the consequences of his own dark fantasy? To be almost destroyed by his obsession/creation? The narrative's consistent refusal of Lisa's point of view leaves us to interpret only the consequences, not the motivations, of her behavior.[40]

Contrary to Allen's assertion, we do know quite a bit about Lisa's motivations, one of which is to get Jeff to agree to a future with her. Perhaps the fact that he has started to privilege "female intuition" isn't enough. Lisa's actions here indicate that he must also see the danger to himself in his earlier wish to be free of women.

LISA: I'm going to make this a week you'll never forget.

In the very same year that *Life* magazine declared the year of "the domestication of the American man," Hitchcock created a film in which a male professional photographer confined to the domestic sphere loses the power to motivate the camera's look on his own, even as he tries to augment that power with longer and longer lenses that humorously caricaturize his phallic quest. Jeff can only achieve his desire to solve a murder through his cooperation with and reliance upon the looks and actions of women. By succumbing to feminization, he actually achieves a certain agency denied to him earlier when he could only see through male eyes. Lisa teaches Jeff to *use* his feminization rather than to resent it. This is the "trade" they make. ("I'll trade you my feminine intuition for a bed for the night.") She gets him and he gets an agency born of her feminine intuition that, ironically, remasculinizes him. And it is a "trade" they make at her suggestion, making her the film's presiding agent. Furthermore, it was Hitchcock himself who granted Lisa this power, albeit somewhat reluctantly. During his cameo, when he parallels Lisa's envious look at the Song Writer, he reveals his wish to identify with and draw on the very power he makes her deny both in that earlier scene ("Where does a man get inspiration to write a song like that?") and in the final scene where she is made to hide her professional interests from Jeff.

Modleski and others don't see the full extent of Lisa's power, arguing of the film's final scene that Lisa's jeans and loafers are a sign that she has capitulated to Jeff's world. Modleski argues that by putting Lisa in jeans, the film "has revealed Jeff to be unable to care for Lisa except insofar as she affirms and mirrors him. . . ."[41] Similarly, critics see Lisa's surreptitious turn from *Beyond the High Himalayas* to *Harper's Bazaar* as a return to a *personal* interest in fashion, an interest that marks her as a woman interested only in how she looks. And yet such an account of the film's ending ignores the fact that, like model-turned-businesswoman Anita Colby, Lisa has a *business* relationship with *Harper's Bazaar,* a relationship she mentioned when she described her day as including a meeting with "the *Harper's Bazaar* people." She ends the film with her professional desires intact and her personal goals fulfilled.

To be sure, there are negative implications for women in the film's final and very pat scene, in addition to the fact that Lisa has to hide her professional desires. Anna Thorwald's murderer may have been revealed, but her life is completely effaced, first through her murder and then, in the film's final scene, by the cleansing of her blood from her apartment's walls. Mrs. Newlywed is doomed to misery, as evidenced by her nagging complaints and her husband's dismissal of them. And although Miss Lonely Hearts and Miss Torso seem to have found the companionship they desire, Miss Lonely Hearts' physical distance from the Song Writer and his own self-centeredness undermine any certainty of a happy ending for her, while Miss Torso's coupling with a man who turns straight to the refrigerator, albeit funny, hints at future dissatisfaction.

But it is also the case that the camera does not allow us to linger on all of these negative implications. It pans from the courtyard to the sleeping Jefferies and finally to the woman who has garnered the power to watch over him. Whereas the opening of the film showed us Jeff in the same sleeping position but alone, accompanied only by the negative of a woman's glamorous pho-

tograph, the film ends with Jeff next to a woman not only power-
fully real but also just plain powerful.

For their help with earlier drafts, I thank John Belton, Audrey Fisch,
Lynn Mahoney, Charles Ponce de Leon, Jim Taylor, and Louise Yelin.

NOTES

1. This tradition began with Jean Douchet's "Hitch and His Public,"
   New York Film Bulletin 7 (1961). See in particular Robert Stam and
   Roberta Pearson, "Hitchcock's *Rear Window:* Reflexivity and the Critique of Voyeurism," *Enclitic* 7, No. 1 (Spring 1983), 136–145.
2. Furthermore, as Scott Curtis notes, the width and height of the
   Thorwalds' windows are the same ratio as CinemaScope. See his
   article in this volume.
3. For clear and concise presentations of psychoanalytic theory and
   psychoanalytic film theory respectively, readers may wish to con-
   sult Terry Eagleton's *Literary Theory: An Introduction* (Minneapolis:
   University of Minnesota Press, 1983), or the section on psychoanalysis in Robert Stam, Robert Burgoyne, and Sandy Flitterman-
   Lewis, *New Vocabularies in Film Semiotics: Structuralism, Post-Struc-
   turalism, and Beyond* (London and New York: Routledge, 1992).
4. Laura Mulvey, "Visual Pleasure and Narrative Cinema," *Screen* 16,
   No. 3 (1975), 6–18.
5. Mulvey never refers to the Oedipus Complex as such. But her
   description of what she calls the "castration complex" indicates
   that she means the same thing. She says of the "castration complex" that it is "essential for the organization of entrance to the
   symbolic order and the law of the order" (13).
6. Ibid., 8.
7. Ibid., 9.
8. Ibid., 10.
9. Robin Wood, *Hitchcock's Films Revisited* (New York: Columbia University Press, 1989), 376.
10. Mulvey, 12. Her model fails to account for homoerotic looking.
11. Ibid., 13–14.
12. Ibid., 15–16.
13. Mulvey herself revisited her position in a 1981 article titled "After-
   thoughts on 'Visual Pleasure and Narrative Cinema' Inspired by
   Duel in the Sun," *Framework* 15–17 (1981), 12–15. She argued there
   that the female spectator oscillates between her "proper" feminine
   and therefore passive path and regression to what Mulvey deems a
   masculine phase of development: "The memory of the 'masculine'
   phase has its own romantic attraction, a last ditch resistance, in
   which the power of masculinity can be used as postponement
   against the power of patriarchy" (15).

14. Tania Modleksi, *The Women Who Knew Too Much: Hitchcock and Feminist Theory* (New York: Methuen, 1988), 76.

15. Due to the large scope of her argument about classical Hollywood cinema, Mulvey devotes only one paragraph to *Rear Window*. That Tania Modleski so stridently takes Mulvey to task for her reading of *Rear Window* – implying that Mulvey is not an "astute" critic of the film – thus seems somewhat unfair.

16. Ibid., 80.

17. Thomas Hine, *Populux: The Look of Life of America in the '50s and '60s, from Tailfins and TV Dinners to Barbie Dolls and Fallout Shelters* (New York: Alfred A. Knopf, 1989), 24.

18. Ibid., 38.

19. For a good history of masculinity in the United States, see Michael Kimmel, *Manhood in America: A Cultural History* (New York: The Free Press, 1996).

20. Ibid., 136.

21. Quoted in ibid., 182.

22. James T. Patterson, *Grand Expectations. The United States, 1945–1974* (New York and Oxford: Oxford University Press, 1996), 32, 34.

23. See, for example, Robert Corber, *In the Name of National Security: Hitchcock, Homophobia, and the Political Construction of Gender in Postwar America* (Durham, NC: Duke University Press, 1993), and Jeanne Allen, "Looking Through 'Rear Window': Hitchcock's Traps and Lures of Heterosexual Romance," in *Female Spectators: Looking at Film and Television,* ed. E. Deidre Pribram (London and New York: Verso, 1988), 31–43. Both assume Lisa is a model. A few, like Sarah Street, assume she is a fashion editor. See her article in this volume.

24. According to the archival work of Steven De Rosa, the deposition was made during a legal battle over the rights of the Woolrich story. It is now sealed.

25. Much of my information on Colby comes from Michael Gross, *Model: The Ugly Business of Beautiful Woman* (New York: William Morrow and Company, Inc., 1996), 48–53, 69–73. See, too, the reprint in Gross of a photograph of Colby and her sister, Francine Counihan, in which Anita's blond hair is strikingly similar to Kelly's in *Rear Window*. Colby can also be seen playing herself in the 1944 Technicolor musical *Cover Girl,* starring Rita Hayworth and Gene Kelly.

26. Gross, 49.

27. Hitchcock may very well have met Colby the year she was featured in *Time,* if not at other times. He was shooting Bergman in *Notorious* (1946).

28. The interview is recorded in Gross, 69–73.

29. Ibid., 50.

30. Arlene Skolnick, *Embattled Paradise: The American Family in the Age of Uncertainty* (New York: Basic Books, 1991), 71.

31. Quoted in Barbara Ehrenreich, *The Hearts of Men: American Dreams and the Flight from Commitment* (New York: Doubleday, 1983), 47.
32. Ibid., 51.
33. As Jeanne Allen explains, "stepped camera" is an optical effect created by duplicating single frames a second time on the filmstrip. The result looks like slow motion but is not as smooth, so that the shot looks more subjective. Allen takes this to mean that Lisa is presented here as a product of Jeff's fantasy (38). But we should not forget either that Lisa initiates this kiss nor that she looms over him during it.
34. See Street, in this volume.
35. For a good discussion of perceptions of female sexuality in the fifties, see "Monroe and Sexuality" in Richard Dyer, *Heavenly Bodies: Film Stars and Society* (New York: St. Martin's Press, 1986).
36. Elaine Tyler May, "Explosive Issues: Sex, Women, and the Bomb." In *Recasting America: Culture and Politics in the Age of Cold War,* ed. Lary May (Chicago and London: University of Chicago Press, 1989), 154–170.
37. Modleski, 78.
38. This is the reverse of Hitchcock's *Notorious,* a film Modleski discusses along these very lines.
39. *Beyond the High Himalayas* was published by Doubleday in 1952. Its author, William O. Douglas (1898–1980), was an avid naturalist but was best known, for the 36 years he served, as a champion of civil liberties on the U.S. Supreme Court, where his term as associate justice is still the longest to date. In June 1953, he faced impeachment charges when he granted a stay of execution to Julius and Ethel Rosenberg, who had been convicted of passing atomic secrets to the Soviet Union. The Rosenbergs were executed on June 19, 1953.
    Hitchcock received the first treatment of *Rear Window* in April 1953 and is listed as a producer of the film as early as May of that year. (See Curtis.) It would be interesting to trace the point at which Hitchcock decided to feature Douglas's book in the last shot of his film and, from there, to examine not only his motivation for doing so but also the way in which Douglas's presence in the shot inflects its meaning as well as that of the overall film. *Rear Window* is, after all, a film about spying and accusation, topics that kept Americans riveted to the Rosenberg trial during the spring of 1953.
40. Allen, 39.
41. Modleski, 84.

3 "The Dresses Had Told Me"

FASHION AND FEMININITY IN *REAR WINDOW*

"They were a woman's dresses, and he was pulling them down to him one by one, taking the topmost one each time. . . . I knew what it was now, and what he was doing. The dresses had told me. He confirmed it for me."[1] The Cornell Woolrich short story on which *Rear Window* was based deploys costume at a key point as Jeff becomes more and more curious about Lars Thorwald and his invalid wife whose dresses are being packed into a trunk, possibly for a trip, but later confirming her mysterious disappearance. Apart from this notable incidence of costume being used to substantiate Jeff's eventual conclusion that Mrs. Thorwald has been murdered, the short story does not feature costume or accessories as significant character, plot, or symbolic devices. The dresses tell a simple story. Hitchcock's *Rear Window,* on the other hand, displays clothing on many occasions, functioning as a complex system. Intriguing possibilities are created for all the characters via their costumes, particularly Lisa (Grace Kelly) who does not appear in the short story but whose dresses, bags, and jewels tell a fascinating story that far exceeds the simple imperatives of plot development. This chapter discusses five major areas in which the film's costumes and accessories perform significant roles: narrative development, the delineation of gender relations, the articulation of the class theme, star images and the development of the "masquerading blonde," and finally the role of costume in the film's authorship.

In terms of the basic advancement of the narrative, accessories

are central to the thriller plot on several occasions: Jeff sees Thorwald remove jewels and rings from his wife's reddish-brown handbag, an action that is confirmed as highly suspicious according to
Lisa's theory based on "feminine intuition" that no woman would
go on a trip without her favorite handbag, jewels, and especially her
wedding ring. Mrs. Thorwald's bag is given importance from our
first introduction to her when it hangs on her bedpost. After her
disappearance, it stands in for her when Thorwald rummages
through it and again when Lisa holds it upside down to show Jeff
and Stella that the jewels have disappeared. When Lisa further
explores Thorwald's apartment, her retrieval of the wedding ring
appears to confirm Jeff's suspicion that Mrs. Thorwald must have
been murdered. The investment of props with important narrative
functions is not unusual in Hitchcock, and in this case provides a
useful link between the thriller and romance plots. Lisa's attain-
ment of the wedding ring provides closure on two counts: It confirms Thorwald's guilt and demonstrates Lisa's bravery, thus proving
her worthiness of a place in Jeff's masculine world of adventure.[2]

On a general level, *Rear Window* utilizes costume as a way of
identifying character traits about the occupants of the apartments
Jeff spends his days gazing into. The theme of looking and appearance is prominent, particularly in that most of the scenes involving Jeff's neighbors are silent; we learn about them primarily from
costume and other elements of mise-en-scène. The first person we
see in any detail in the apartments opposite Jeff's is the composer,
who is wearing an undershirt and pajama bottoms looking tired,
unfit, and overweight. He resolutely turns off a radio program that
is giving fitness tips and we gradually shift attention to Miss
Torso's apartment where her trim figure and almost constant exercise routines contrast with the sluggish composer.[3] Our first peek
at her is through her bathroom window, facing away from us. She
then walks into the main room, fastening her pink bra which
matches her shorts. She is equipped for physical exercise but also
for Jeff's gaze as he looks on with approval, adopting a wry smile
as he surveys her smooth, gyrating body movements while she
completes simple domestic tasks. Also contrasted with the ever-

popular Miss Torso is Miss Lonely Hearts who is middle-aged, wears green (an unlucky color),[4] entertains imaginary guests, has poor eyesight, and needs a stiff drink before she can face the world. A state of undress/nightwear can indicate vulnerability, as in the case of Mrs. Thorwald and her "double" in pajamas, Jeff.[5] Jeff's pajamas signify his status as a patient, incarcerated in his apartment, at the mercy of the women who visit him, and subject to disbelief by Doyle who questions his judgment on several occasions. Lisa's nightgown is not as threatening to Jeff as her black dress, and it is significant that the nightgown appears once her sexual assertiveness has been contained by her recruitment into Jeff's murder-mystery scenario.

The major role performed by costume, however, concerns gender relations, particularly the central conflict between Lisa and Jeff. Jeff is immobilized after an accident when he was hit by a fly-away wheel while trying to photograph a racing car as it crashed. The film gives several indications that Jeff is experiencing a crisis of his masculinity: He fears that he may have lost his nerve and dreads the prospect of perhaps having to give up his action-photography (and parka hanging on his door) in favor of Lisa's lucrative world of high fashion where he would have to don a dark blue flannel suit. We know he has already been lured in that direction because at the beginning of the film we see two photographs of a model, one negative and one positive, the latter adorning the cover of a magazine. This photograph presumably was taken by Jeff and stands awkwardly next to his photographs of crashing racing cars. There are other indications that Jeff is far from the fearless creature he used to be: He can't uncork the wine bottle; he is squeamish when Stella talks of dismemberment and can't eat his food despite chiding Lisa for never having eaten "fishheads and rice"; his dialogue is often stuttering and hesitant; he is terrified of Thorwald; he looks but does not act, failing to take even one photograph that would surely help to corroborate his story. The plaster cast on his leg symbolizes Jeff's crisis of masculinity and also conveys his weakness in identity, a point that is further signified by the scrawled initials on the cast that resemble an inscription on a tombstone. ("Here lie the broken bones of L. B. Jefferies.") His state of undress therefore underlines the theme of Jeff's vulnerability, and his further disablement at the end of the film when both of his legs are broken means that his masculinity remains in question and that he will remain "vulnerable" for a considerable period of time.[6]

Lisa's costumes and accessories display a resolute assertion of her femininity. Far from being passive, Lisa is an extremely active character, dominating many scenes with her mobility. She is also photographed from camera angles that convey the extent to which she is a both a physical and an emotional threat to Jeff. Her two major scenes begin with a close-up of her face, kissing Jeff and dominating the frame. Her knowledge of fashion and awareness of her clothed body as feminine spectacle invest Lisa with power over her image, the power of performance and of masquerade, which underscore issues of sexual difference. As Tania Modleski has commented: "In *Rear Window* 'fashion' is far from representing woman's unproblematic assimilation to the patriarchal system, but functions to some extent as a signifier of feminine desire and difference."[7] During the film Lisa wears six different outfits, accompanied by numerous bags and jewels which serve as signifiers of feminine desire and difference, constituting a discourse of particular significance to female spectators. In keeping with her classy, monied image, she wears her different costumes to suit particular times of the day: She knows what outfit to wear, when to wear it, and how to display it with greatest impact.

Lisa's entrance is marked by a particularly theatrical performance, assisted by the camera's increasing distance in three movements, each time giving us more of Lisa as she turns on one after another light until our vision of her is complete: "Lisa . . . Carol . . . Fremont." Her outfit is a black, tight-fitting top with a full, white layered net skirt, and a white chiffon shawl worn with a pearl choker. The overall style for Lisa's costumes, particularly her evening wear, is the "New Look," the style launched in Paris in 1947 which celebrated full, feminine skirts and placed particular emphasis on the body's contours. This particular outfit is interesting because it encapsulates the broad spectrum of femininity that is evident in many of Lisa's other outfits and, indeed, in her overall "look." The tight black top connotes a ballerina's athleticism while the full skirt and shawl present her femininity as a full, larger-than-life construct. Hitchcock's decision to introduce her to us "in bits" has a fascinating cumulative impact that would not have had the same force if we had simply seen her in a single shot. Instead we see her in close-up and then there is more, and more, and more of her. She is the epitomy of New Look couture, tempered by a hint of the androgynous, sleek image associated with Audrey Hepburn that had been popular in the early 1950s. In terms of Kelly's star image it is worth remembering her family background and its association with sporting activities: Her father was an Olympic oarsman and her mother a champion swimmer (and former cover girl). Indeed, Lisa later proves that she can be athletic when she shinnies up a ladder and nimbly climbs from the balcony through the window and into the main room of Thorwald's apartment. But Lisa's potential as an action-girl is always qualified by her excessive femininity which at times overwhelms Jeff so much that he recoils in horror. In terms of the film's theme of gender conflict, it is interesting to note that the New Look was very much a reaction to the more masculine, box-shouldered styles that prevailed during wartime austerity. In a recent study of popular British films in the late 1940s, Pam Cook noted how their adoption of New Look fashions was the cause of considerable anxiety: "The New Look aroused primitive fears about female sexuality: both women and men dreaded being swallowed up by an overwhelming maternal body."[8] These remarks might well apply to Jeff's predicament, which is most acute when Lisa wears her second outfit, a full, black dress that signifies only one thing: seduction. The dress has a full skirt and short sleeves and is low-cut with a thinner layer of translucent black material on the top that exposes both shoulders.

This costume is Lisa's most threatening and she wears it after their apparent marital incompatibility has been discussed without resolution. Hitchcock always favored the use of "quiet" colors –

eau de nile, grays, and greens – unless a particularly dramatic effect was required, as in this case.[9] She is wearing the black dress when they have their second kiss after which Jeff tries to get Lisa interested in the Thorwald mystery. Throughout the following dialogue Lisa is kissing Jeff whenever she can, nuzzling his neck with her eyes closed, desperately trying to get him to concentrate on her, while Jeff is rather passive, backing off from her advances whenever possible. The dialogue itself is interesting because it hints at Lisa's dissatisfaction with Jeff as a man, almost insinuating that his obsession with Thorwald is sexual:

LISA: How far does a girl have to go before you notice her?

JEFF: Well, if she's pretty enough she doesn't have to go anywhere, she just has to *be*.

LISA: Well, ain't I? Pay attention to me.

JEFF: Well, I'm . . . I'm . . . I'm not exactly on the other side of the room.

LISA: Um, your mind is and when I want a man I want all of him.

JEFF: Don't . . . don't you ever have any problems?

LISA: Um . . . I have one right now.

JEFF: So do I.

LISA: Tell me about it.

JEFF: Why . . . why would a man leave his apartment three times on a rainy night with a suitcase? And come back three times?

LISA: He likes the way his wife welcomes him home.

JEFF: No, no, no, no, no, no – not this salesman's wife. And why didn't he go to work today?

LISA: Homework. It's more interesting.

JEFF: What's . . . what's interesting about a butcher knife and a small saw wrapped up in newspaper, huh?

LISA: Nothing, thank heaven.

JEFF: Why hasn't he been in his wife's bedroom all day?

LISA: I wouldn't dare answer that.

JEFF: Listen, I'll answer and tell you . . . there's something terribly wrong.

LISA: And I'm afraid it's with me.

JEFF: What do you think?

LISA: Something too frightful to utter.

JEFF: He went out a few minutes ago in his undershirt and hasn't come back yet.

This key scene shifts attention away from the marriage question which dominated Jeff's previous interactions with Lisa, although it is clear that Lisa can only interpret Jeff's remarks with it in mind. He manages to counter her sexual challenge and interest her in the murder scenario; by the end of the scene she is begging to learn everything he saw and what he thinks it means.

Lisa's third outfit is an almond green silk linen suit, smart and businesslike, chic but with a more tailored, masculine shape than her two previous costumes. The skirt is narrow, below the knee with a short matching box jacket and a white, backless halter blouse and white gloves. Once again, her jewels are predominantly pearls; her hair is up and she is wearing a smart, pillbox hat. She is presented as ready for the job of detecting, on the Thorwald case with Jeff, inviting herself to stay the night so that she too can see "everything" opposite. But once again her image is riddled with contradictions where "femininity" appears to be a multifaceted construction, capable of revealing itself in different guises but never showing all. The greenish hue of the suit provides a color link with Miss Lonely Hearts, symbolic perhaps of a deeper affinity between the two women recognized by Lisa but rejected by Jeff as nonsense. Her jewels jangle and distract from the seriousness of her initial appearance, and when she removes her jacket the sleeveless halter blouse reveals her bare arms, another example of how a sense of sexual presence is concealed but later revealed. The pièce de résistance of this fascinating composite is her smart, black Mark Cross overnight case which contains ultra-feminine nightwear, a white gown with silk slippers.

The overnight case is an excellent example of the handbag as a sexual symbol. In many Hitchcock films a woman's handbag functions as a private space, often concealing secrets or evidence of multiple identities.[10] Lisa's overnight case looks as if it is a business case, but when she opens it, out cascades the white nightgown and the slippers, an excessive revelation of feminine clothing that has obvious sexual connotations. Hitchcock appears to be drawing on Freudian notions of a woman's handbag being symbolic of the vagina and of masturbatory activity, a power symbol of her ability to control her own sexuality.[11] As with other Hitchcock films that feature handbags in relation to femininity and sexuality, Lisa has particular control over her bag (and hence her sexuality) as a single woman. Compare Lisa's usage of her bag in *Rear Window* with the far more restrictive use allowed for the married Margot (also played by Grace Kelly) in *Dial "M" for Murder* (1954). In *Rear Window*, Lisa's bag is "hers"; she controls it. In *Dial "M" for Murder*, Margot's handbag is repeatedly invaded by her husband, who has not only stolen a love letter from her bag but also pilfers her latchkey from it. Interestingly, Mrs. Thorwald's reddish-brown bag resembles Margot's; both are married women who are in danger from their husbands who rifle through their handbags. Mrs. Thorwald's empty bag is unlike Lisa's Mark Cross case which bursts open in a display of feminine excess. Although Jeff and Doyle are consumed with curiosity at the sight of Lisa's bag, with its associations of feminine mystique and masquerade, it is hard to imagine them rifling through it with the temerity of Thorwald.

The single "masquerading blonde" who appeared in many subsequent Hitchcock films frequently used her bag in an intriguing manner, often signifying independence and transgression. Lisa herself appears to recognize the transgressive possibilities when she notices Doyle's surprised expression when he sees the bag and nightwear, later asking Jeff whether Doyle thinks she stole the case.[12] Having earlier remarked playfully to Jeff about the case – "I'll bet yours isn't this small" – in further comic, sexually suggestive fashion, Lisa's bag is contrasted with Jeff's enormous phallic lens as he comments on her "feminine intuition" as "inside stuff," while she immediately counters his observation with a more assertive description: "It's basic equipment." Basic equipment indeed for the fifties woman who used fashion knowingly, capable of performing a "masquerade" of femininity that demonstrated her survival instinct in a male-dominated world.[13]

It is interesting to contemplate at this stage to what extent Lisa's white nightgown represents her promise of a "preview of coming attractions." As her fourth outfit, the nightgown is actually less threatening than the black dress with which Lisa so des-

Thorwald (Raymond Burr) goes through Mrs. Thorwald's handbag while consulting with someone on the telephone as to its contents. Photo courtesy of the British Film Institute.

perately tried to seduce Jeff. As I remarked earlier, the nightgown provides a link between Lisa and Mrs. Thorwald: Although it is full and feminine, it also renders the women vulnerable to male control, while of course from Jeff's point of view it creates a disturbing link between Lisa and Mrs. Thorwald, who is portrayed as a nagging wife. Jeff's most anxious sexual moment with Lisa has, however, passed, and her attention has now shifted to the Thorwald case. The narrative does not allow Lisa to use the nightgown as a seductive device: As soon as she has put it on, Jeff's attention is distracted from it by the courtyard incident of the dog's death when all the neighbors except Thorwald look out of their windows. Thereafter the film's narrative shifts more and more attention to the murder as Stella is also recruited into Jeff's amateur detective team. The precise nature of the "attractions" Lisa might have in store for Jeff are therefore unclear at this stage and remain

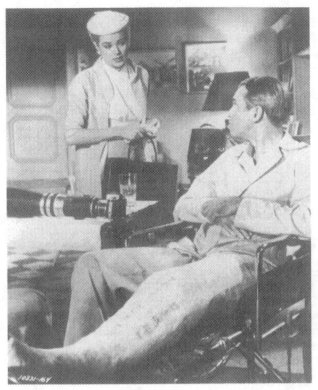

Jeff (Stewart) and Lisa (Grace Kelly) both have "inside stuff." Jeff's "basic equipment" is a camera outfitted with a telephoto lens; Lisa's is a Mark Cross overnight bag packed with a nightgown and slippers. Photo courtesy of the British Film Institute.

so at the film's closure which provides an enigmatic representation of "the feminine."

The next costume change for Lisa into an afternoon dress is appropriate for her role as an intrepid action-woman, but as with her other outfits it is in the height of fashion featuring a bouncy, fullish skirt. Her patterned white silk organdy print in wheat-colored spring flowers is practical and unfussy. It resembles Stella's sensible dresses which look like uniforms. The main difference is that Stella's are from the mid-1940s while Lisa's are the latest variations on a classic style. Stella's dress is brown with a uniform pat-

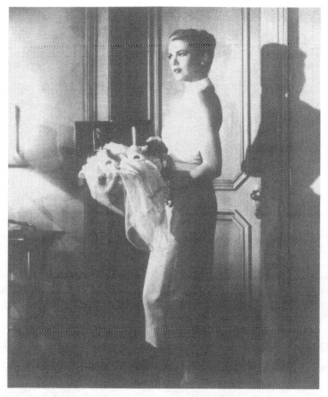

Lisa displays the contents of her bag and describes them as a "preview of coming attractions." Photo courtesy of the British Film Institute.

tern and V-neck, generally exuding a more utilitarian appearance than Lisa's, which is waisted with a high neckline. Both, however, are definitely "day dresses," a similarity that emphasises their new roles as Jeff's accomplices in the investigation. Lisa's dress does not get in the way when she climbs through the window of Thorwald's apartment and does not encourage an impression of her as a sexual being to anything like the same extent as her previous costumes.

Lisa's final outfit is often interpreted as evidence that she has succumbed to Jeff's masculine world, with her secret peek at *Harper's Bazaar* suggesting that her love of fashion will never be completely erased. What she is wearing bears this out: a highly coutured pair of slacks, a pink shirt, and sensible, but obviously very expensive, shoes. This outfit raises many intriguing possibilities for the film's discussion of gender. It is often assumed that Jeff responds to Lisa only when she proves that she can survive in a dangerous situation, providing Jeff with an element of "narcissistic projection" that her previous "performances" have not allowed.[14] But the film's ambivalent closure raises the question: Will Lisa really abandon her fashion career to join Jeff on his expeditions and would he actually want her to accompany him? Her bravery has proved that she has guts, but in the light of Jeff's own crisis of masculinity it is feasible that he would prefer her to be out of the way until he has recovered his own nerve. Lisa has demontrated that she likes adventure and so would probably not be prepared to sit back and wait for him to come back from his adventures. Her active role in the frame *and* in the narrative is indeed a "preview of coming attractions," although for Jeff the "attractions" in question – female assertiveness and independence – might not be so appealing. From this standpoint Lisa is a double threat to Jeff in her ultrafeminine costumes *and* her guise as an action-woman: Both paralyze him with anxiety about his own masculinity.

Costume is an indicator of class in *Rear Window,* a theme that, as Janet Staiger has pointed out, has hardly been broached in previous analyses.[15] Lisa's world of fashion represents an upper-middle-class milieu: She works as a magazine fashion editor and mixes in society circles.[16] By contrast, Jeff is a hard-working reporter who lives in a small, downscale Greenwich Village apartment, resisting Lisa's attempts to render him "upwardly mobile" by securing him a full-time job as a studio fashion photographer. Lisa's representation of class is largely based on taste: During her first scene she tells Jeff that she wants to exchange his "cracked . . . ornate and gaudy" cigarette box for a plain silver one, engraved with his initials. Her outfits are in impeccable taste and her knowledge of fashion is impressive. As far as professionalism is concerned, she and Jeff are equally dedicated to their jobs, although Jeff's

repeated dismissal of her job as frivolous and rather amusing con-
fers a higher status on his own profession. Lisa is extremely con-
scientious about her work, trying out clothes in the evenings and
speaking animatedly about professional events she has attended,
recollecting details about gowns worn by the rich and famous
with enthusiasm and accuracy. Similarly, Jeff says that he took
some of his best photographs on his "days off," including the
unfortunate car race. In many ways, therefore, Lisa's "perfection"
is about her professionalism as a working woman, ambition and
enthusiasm for her job being a consistent theme in the film.
Again, it is interesting to note how Lisa's status as a single woman
invests her display of costume with professional *and* personal sat-
isfaction, strictly departing from Veblen's critique of costume as
an element of conspicuous consumption, particularly among middle-class wives whose costumes showed off their husbands'
wealth.[17] Instead, as I have argued, Lisa's costumes are conspicuous
in the sense that they suggest a persona that revolves around
notions of the "feminine" that suggest independence, assertiveness, and survival.

Miss Lonely Hearts is represented as being of lower class than
Lisa by her costumes and particularly by their degree of color satu-
ration. In many ways Miss Lonely Hearts is a vulgar version of Lisa,
often performing similar actions but her actions, are signified as
cheaper and sadder. When Miss Lonely Hearts leaves her apartment
to go to the bar where she picks up a young man, she is wearing a
brash, relatively high-saturated green dress. By contrast, the suit
Lisa wears when she comes to spend the night in Jeff's apartment is
a pastel shade of green, somehow more refined, less vulgar, made of
softer, finer-textured material, and in keeping with her aristocratic
upper East Side demeanor. Stella's sensible shoes and practical,
unfussy dresses confirm her status as a working-class nurse with
down-to-earth common sense. Stella's dress indicates her lower-
income bracket, particularly the regular polka-dot pattern and the
relative dark value of its brown color. Her stable position in the
film's narrative as wise arbiter between Jeff and Lisa, and then as
their comedic accomplice in the murder-mystery, does not require

her to adopt many changes of character or costume, although the patterns of her dresses vary from time to time. Lisa's literal and figurative mobility therefore contrasts with Stella's stereotypical casting and with Jeff's physical immobility and his determination not to be upwardly mobile on the social scale. Stella represents a fixed image of the working-class woman, and her dresses do not make Jeff anxious from a social or sexual perspective.

A discussion of class in *Rear Window* leads naturally into Grace Kelly's star image at the time of the film's release, which was very much based on the idea of her as "a lady." The press referred to Kelly's Philadelphia origins and family life which was wealthy and secure, stressing middle-class norms of hard work by mentioning her father's humble background and one-time job as a bricklayer.[18] Her pre–*Rear Window* image was of the ice cool, classy blonde, and Hitchcock's stated aim for her was to surprise the audience by bringing out a repressed sense of passionate sexuality.[19] Her previous film roles (prior to *Dial "M" for Murder*) had not exuded this, and even after Hitchcock had combined her "ladylike" qualities with sexuality, some fan magazines still preferred to discuss her as somewhat distant, patrician, genteel, and reserved. Thomas Harris examined a wide range of articles on Grace Kelly and Marilyn Monroe between 1951 and 1956, observing that there was never much direct reportage from Kelly herself "as if it would be beneath her dignity to discuss topics which made Marilyn Monroe a household name. Yet a careful balance was maintained lest the impression be conveyed that Miss Kelly was aloof from her fellows."[20] She can be usefully compared with other stars whose images were similarly founded on class and elegance: Katharine Hepburn, Audrey Hepburn, and in Britain, Anna Neagle. A British reporter who interviewed Kelly in New York in December 1954 predicted that the "Kelly look" would eclipse Audrey Hepburn's waif-like androgyny. On the other hand, magazines such as *Confidential* reported gossip about Kelly's alleged affair with Ray Milland during the filming of *Dial "M" for Murder,* and Hedda Hopper accused Kelly of causing a rift between Milland and his wife that almost resulted in divorce. Despite Kelly's denial of the affair the

Lisa and Stella (Ritter) in their "day dresses." Photo courtesy of the British Film Institute.

New York Journal American referred to her as "an off-screen jinx domestic-wise to her leading men."[21] This dual image of the classy blonde who exuded smoldering sexuality was therefore reflected in the press and in *Rear Window.*

In terms of costume, Edith Head's challenge was to strike the correct balance between Kelly as a film star and Lisa as a character in *Rear Window,* inviting the viewer to maintain a firm idea of the star underneath the clothes but at the same time be "shocked" by the character who might contradict some of the star's well-known qualities. As Jane Gaines has put it: "The ideal in this way becomes the transformation of the star that plays on a fascination with masquerade while remaining a transformation that stops short of complete disguise."[22] Consequently, the narrative of *Rear Window* might function in such a way for spectators that an absence of Lisa's "backstory" could be supplied by the image of Grace Kelly that contained the above contradictory elements: It does not matter that we don't know much about Lisa because we can imagine something very similar to Grace Kelly's well-known background. On the other hand, viewers who preferred to think of Kelly as regal, cool, and dignified might indeed be "shocked" at Lisa's sexual advances toward Jeff and the coded sexual symbolism of items like handbags and camera lenses. *Rear Window*'s overall fascination with masquerade and performance should be seen in the context of Hitchcock's consistent subsequent use of blonde actresses like Grace Kelly, including Kim Novak, "Tippi" Hedren, and Janet Leigh, who on the surface appeared to be conformist but who also had immense transgressive potential.

The role of costume in *Rear Window* raises interesting questions about the film's authorship. Hitchcock notoriously controlled every aspect of his films, a point he made much of in interviews – actors, actresses, and technicians appearing to be mere putty in the hands of the great *auteur*. Edith Head designed Grace Kelly's costumes for the first time in *Rear Window* and often said that Hitchcock was extremely precise as to particular colors: "There was a reason for every color, every style and he was absolutely certain about everything he settled on. . . . Hitch wanted her to appear like a piece of Dresden china, something slightly untouchable."[23] On other occasions Head admitted that Hitchcock allowed her considerable say, particularly regarding styles and in negotiating with actresses about appropriate accessories.[24] Head recalled that designing for Kelly was a special experience because she was so knowledgeable about fashion: "You show her fabrics and she discusses them with you like a professional. She knows the difference between a hoop skirt and a crinoline. She is a very well-informed person."[25] The collaboration of Head and Hitchcock in this way suggests that feminine input into the film's costuming was crucial and that the precision of each outfit, its resonances, and intertextual associations would have constituted a key focus point, particularly for female audiences.

The story told by the dresses in *Rear Window* privileges Lisa as an active, masquerading, and threatening figure. Hitchcock, Edith Head, and Grace Kelly were offering a representation of femininity that was consistent with contemporary discussions about the aggressive nature of female sexuality. Increased knowledge and publicity about women's sexual desires, from the Kinsey Report for example, shattered previously held ideas about women as passive, nonsexual creatures whose fascination for men depended upon their being shrouded in "feminine mystique."[26] In 1954 the mystique was being exploded, and *Rear Window* displays all the inherent tensions of that moment between demystifying femininity and at the same time employing it in the traditional sense as an enigma. Lisa knows too much about women, more than Jeff can take. She represents an "excess" of femininity that we can see from her various ironic, masquerading performances. She shamelessly flits between the fullsome, feminine fashions of the New Look and the more tailored, masculine style of her final masquerade, encompassing a schizophrenic couture that reflects the period's anxiety about gender roles. Lisa is threatening to Jeff as an excessively feminine woman and also as an active figure who proves her bravery at a time when Jeff's own masculinity is in crisis. In the scene quoted earlier in which Lisa wears a black seduction dress, she asks Jeff how far a girl has to go to be noticed. He replies that she does not have to go anywhere if she is pretty enough, she "just has to *be*." In *Rear Window* Lisa does much more than "just *be*." In her various costumes and accessories she performs, suggests, *and* disturbs.

I would like to thank John Belton and Sue Simkin for their astute comments on drafts of this chapter.

NOTES

1. Cornell Woolrich's short story *Rear Window*, reprinted in David Wheeler, ed., *No, But I Saw the Movie* (London: Penguin, 1989), 350–351.
2. Although at another level, the film's closure is highly ambivalent.
3. It is interesting that Hitchcock chose to make his personal appear-

ance in the composer's apartment, presumably identifying with the composer as the "author" of the piece which is completed by the end of the film but also, perhaps, with the composer as an unfit physical specimen!

4. See entry on the color green in Iona Opie and Moira Tatem, eds., *Oxford Dictionary of Superstitions* (Oxford: Oxford University Press, 1996 ed.), 181–182.

5. Tania Modleski makes this interesting connection between Mrs. Thorwald and Jeff in *The Women Who Knew Too Much: Hitchcock and Feminist Theory* (London and New York: Methuen, 1988), 77.

6. This reading is consistent with Stewart's later role as Scottie in *Vertigo* as a former cop who is traumatized when his vertigo leads to the death of a friend. It also should be noted that Jeff has been told that he is too valuable as the magazine's best photographer to be allowed on dangerous missions.

7. Modleski, 78.

8. Pam Cook, *Fashioning the Nation: Costume and Identity in British Cinema* (London: British Film Institute, 1996), 58.

9. Edith Head quoted in David Chierichetti, *Hollywood Costume Design* (London: Cassell and Collier Macmillan, 1976), 71.

10. For a further discussion of Hithcock's use of handbags from *Dial "M" for Murder* to *Marnie*, see Sarah Street, "Hitchcockian Haberdashery," in *Hitchcock Annual*, 1995–96, 23–37.

11. See the case of Dora, "Fragment of an Analysis of a Case of Hysteria," in *The Pelican Freud Library* (Harmondsworth: Penguin, 1973), vol. 8. In this case Dora has a dream in which her mother keeps her jewelcase on her bedpost, an observation that bears uncanny resemblance to Lisa's theory about Mrs. Thorwald and her favorite handbag!

12. Other notable associations between handbags, transgression, and stealing occur in *Psycho* and *Marnie*.

13. I am using "masquerade" here as an elaboration of Joan Riviere's original psychoanalytic conception which is interpreted as subversive within patriarchy by John Fletcher, "Versions of Masquerade," in *Screen*, vol. 29, no. 3 (Summer 1988), and by Mary Ann Doane, *Femmes Fatales: Feminism, Film Theory, Psychoanalysis* (London: Routledge, 1992). An ironic and excessive performance of femininity betrays a sophisticated knowledge of the codes at work in gender construction. "By destabilizing the image, masquerading confounds the masculine structure of the Look, and generates the possibility of the female image being manipulated, produced, and read by women. In other words, the act of putting on femininity with a vengeance suggests also the power of taking it off." See A. Kuhn and S. Radstone, eds., *The Women's Companion to International Film* (London: Virago, 1990), 257.

14. See, for example, Jeanne Allen who argues that "bonding for him occurs only when Lisa is trapped and endangered, ambiguously also

the moment of his greatest narcissistic projection." "Looking Through *Rear Window:* Hitchcock's Traps and Lures of Heterosexual Romance," in E. Diedre Pribram, ed., *Female Spectators: Looking at Film and Television* (London: Verso, 1988), 39.

15. See Janet Staiger's case study on *Rear Window* in *Interpreting Films: Studies in the Historical Reception of American Cinema* (Princeton, NJ: Princeton University Press, 1992), 81–95.

16. I am drawing on the categories of the American class system proposed by William Goldschmidt in 1950: An upper-class elite that was small, based on money, power, and aristocratic orientation in its subculture; the middle class (40%), oriented toward the fiscal elite and hard-working (whereas the upper class favored leisure over employment); manual workers; and the lower class. Quoted in Arthur Marwick, *Class: Image and Reality in Britain, France and the USA Since 1930* (London: Fontana/Collins, 1981), 265.

17. See Jane Gaines's interesting discussion of costume in her introduction to *Fabrications: Costume and the Female Body* (New York: Routledge, 1990), co-edited with Charlotte Herzog.

18. Her uncle, playwright George Kelly, later claimed that Jack Kelly exaggerated his "rags to riches" biography, revealing that he had been assisted by family money in the construction industry and in show business. See Robert Lacey, *Grace* (London: Pan Books, 1995), 30.

19. Hitchcock told Truffaut that he wanted sex on screen to be accompanied by surprise, particularly in the case of Grace Kelly. See Francois Truffaut, *Hitchcock* (London: Panther, 1969 ed.), 277–278.

20. Thomas Harris, "The Building of Popular Images," an article written in 1957 and reprinted in Christine Gledhill, ed., *Stardom: Industry of Desire* (London: Routledge, 1991), 42.

21. Quoted in Jane Ellen Wayne, *The Life and Loves of Grace Kelly* (Oxford: Robson Books, 1992), 110.

22. See Gaines in Gaines and Herzog, eds., 201. Gaines quotes Edith Head's comment that she wanted to "shock" the viewer, making them incredulous that Grace Kelly was acting a particular part.

23. Edith Head quoted in Sarah Bradford, *Princess Grace* (London: Weidenfeld and Nicholson, 1984), 82.

24. See Head: "Other than colors, Hitchcock gives you a lot of room for your own ideas," quoted in Joel Finler, *Alfred Hitchcock: The Hollywood Years* (London: Batsford, 1992), 120. Head and Kelly bought the bags and shoes for *To Catch A Thief* together in Paris.

25. Head interviewed by Gwen Robyns for her book, *Princess Grace* (London: W. H. Allen, 1982), 88.

26. In 1954 Alfred Kinsey published *Sexual Behavior of the Human Female,* a best-selling empirical study that demonstrated that women engaged in, and enjoyed, a far greater degree of sexual activity and experimentation than had previously been assumed.

4 Alfred Hitchcock's Rear Window

THE FOURTH SIDE

One of the principal difficulties in a scenario like that of *Rear Window,* I imagine, was to make the spectators complicit, during the entire film, with the pure voyeurism of the protagonists. This would have been difficult because, except at the end, they are not threatened by the (possible) murderer whose actions they study, nor is it necessary for them to defend anyone, since the crime has already been committed by the time they start to become interested in him.

However, this difficulty is directly confronted at the very beginning of the film, in the first scene between Jeff (James Stewart) and his nurse, Stella (Thelma Ritter). Stella anticipates the spectator's reaction, with an unambiguous condemnation: "We've become a race of Peeping Toms." This condemnation is, in fact, something of an endorsement of voyeurism; Stella herself will be, when the moment arrives, the most enthusiastic participant in this sport and will display the most fertile of morbid fantasies concerning the murder across the way.

On the other hand, there indeed is something that is never said or alluded to throughout the film, and that must not be – because the whole working out of the story depends on its repression. This is the *fourth side* of the city block[1] where Jeff's small apartment is located, because this fourth side must necessarily also have many apartments, from which other people could also observe, just as well as Jeff does, the dramatic events that unfold through the *open window* of the murderer Thorwald's apartment, events such as the moment when Thorwald violently grabs hold of Lisa (Grace Kelly), who has gotten into his apartment, and clearly prepares to do her harm. The scene is shown as if there were only one apartment and one window from which it could be seen. It is as if, across from the three sides of the buildings that we see continually, in close-up and in detail, there was only one apartment – belonging to Jeff.

Let us note also that there are two places in this apartment that we never enter, in which we see Grace Kelly but we do not follow. These are the bathroom and the kitchen, whose doorways open onto the living room from opposite sides.[2]

All this is, of course, justified from the beginning by the film's "rule" of the *point of view of James Stewart:* Jeff's leg in its cast prevents him from walking, and he will not leave this one room. We are not supposed to see more than he sees from there, while we see him – according to the rules that govern identification in cinema, inscribed within that space (the living room) where his glance may roam freely.

In this case, the application of this "rule" of point of view amounts to an invitation to the audience to share the hero's little apartment, while making it forget (just as the film's characters do) that there may be on Jeff's side of the block other apartments, from which one can see just as well and perhaps even better what goes on in Thorwald's place.

There are in the film at least four times when this restricted point of view is enlarged – one instance completely explicit and acknowledged as such, the others more discreet. Let us begin with the latter; they are generally not noticed. The first occurs right at the film's beginning: James Stewart is asleep in his wheelchair, his head covered with sweat resting near the window sill, and *his back is turned to the courtyard.* We see the city of New York awaken to a new day, one of the hot dog-days of summer. Our gaze traverses this space as Stewart might hear it in his sleep, with its echoing din of radio sounds, children's cries, automobile horns, and boat whistles. At the same time, this scene appears as a kind of extension of his dreaming head.

It's in the same position, and in the same state of sleep, that we later find James Stewart for another apparent escape from his point of view; when we see, from his window, Thorwald leaving at dawn with a mysterious woman in black.

There is a certain charm to films that begin with the awakening of a man and that then introduce us to his point of view: I'm thinking of Welles's *The Trial,* Fellini's *City of Women,* and the central section of Rohmer's *The Aviator's Wife,* where it appears that it is the real world that is dreamlike. As a result, one could say that there is not truly an escape from his point of view when the character sleeps while the action either begins or continues without him.

The space of *Rear Window,* then, adopts the completely imaginary form of a cone, whose apex is constituted by the living room (or, if you like, by James Stewart's head while he is lying horizontally, with his back to the window) and then extends out toward its base in the courtyard and in the world beyond that. And it is necessary to keep the spectator forgetful – of the fact that it is impossible that the little apartment could be the only thing that faces this vast cityscape.

There are, however, two moments in the film when we leave the room, and when we are made to see this fourth "forgotten" side. In point of fact, we see it very well at the end, when James Stewart is ejected from the window and falls into the yard below. But because of the very fragmented editing and because of the intensity of the situation, we don't fully realize the implications of this revelation. (And, if my memory doesn't deceive me, there aren't any lighted or lived-in windows on this fourth wall.)

The other moment when "leaving" the apartment is quite apparent, and indeed is made to be noticed, is the scene of the death of the little dog – when the retired, childless couple who live in one of the upper stories discover, at night, the body of their "dear child" stretched out below them on the ground. The cries, tears, and curses of the woman – she screams, "You don't know the meaning of the word 'neighbor.' . . . Did you kill him because he liked you?" – draw everyone to their windows (and balconies). We see the young married couple who desert, for one moment,

The Death of the Dog: All the neighbors come to their balconies or windows except for Thorwald. Note that this moment follows the brief, "objective" disruption of Jeff's point of view discussed in the text. Photo courtesy of Paramount.

the conjugal bed; Miss Lonely Hearts from the ground floor; the guests at the party given by the young composer; and so on (except for Thorwald obviously).

"This, incidentally, is the only moment," says Truffaut to Hitchcock, who agrees, "at which the film changes its point of view. By simply taking the camera outside of Stewart's apartment, the whole scene becomes entirely objective."[3] And, in fact, this is the first time that the tenants opposite the hero's apartment are not seen from far away, not "enlarged" and crushed by the perspective of a long focal length lens, but seen close up, in "normal" perspective, and from angles that, in terms of height, are unlike those we had from Stewart's window. There is also an extraordinary, extremely brief shot, which shows us all of the courtyard in its entirety. All? In fact, only that part of it that faces Stewart's windows, but (almost magically) we believe we saw it *all*, and that is what was meant to happen – in this apparently objective point of view that continues to ignore the existence of the fourth side. And it's very probable that, in its rapid mix of "broken" and dislocated points of view, this sequence of muddled unanimity – which is, all the same, very moving – is there to make us believe that the people in the various apartments come together, and that we see them all, without leaving one the time to construct, to compose, to become conscious of a fourth side.

We could, moreover, ask if an exclusion so radical, and so essential to the functioning of the film, is not without a relation to what Jean-Pierre Oudart, in his article on "Cinema and Suture," said of the conjuring away of the space of the Absent one – a repression that is the very basis for the construction of what he calls "subjective" cinema.[4]

The film's use of sound, about which there could be a great deal to say, obviously contributes to the complete direction of attention in the direction of the courtyard.[5] What is heard – the sound of radios, of barely audible bits of conversations, of children's games, of piano playing, of street and city noises – is devised to be linked to what we see across the way. But there is at least one ambient sound, which plays an all-the-more-secret and important role because it is not attributable to an identifiable tenant across the way – and so it is, in relation to the other sounds, outside of space: the musical scales sung by an invisible female singer. I like to think that this woman's voice brings a free element, escaping all requirement of spatialization, to the localized, everyday fabric of music and noises that arrives from the courtyard as if from an enormous burial pit of sounds.

Moreover, we hear one of these monotonous scales of the invisible singer the first night, just before the silent, impromptu arrival of Grace Kelly – and just before the wonderful, bewildering silence that literally *closes* on the kiss of the two lovers. It is like an ebbtide – so surprising and well prepared – of the sonic materials that have been beating under James Stewart's window since the beginning of the film.

We may see throughout the film that, just as Godard in *Prenom Carmen* "opens" and "closes" at will the sound of the sea, Hitchcock opens and closes freely the noises from the courtyard, depending on his needs.[6] Sometimes this is to attract the attention of James Stewart (and the spectator) to the exterior; sometimes, to the contrary, it is to "close" the dramatic space on the little theater of the living room and on the intimate domesticity of Lisa and Jeff.

The reference to the theater is not even an interpretive act imposed on the film. Grace Kelly herself makes it when, closing the curtain of the living room window and depriving James Stewart of his spectacle, she promises him a compensation; she offers herself as a "coming attraction."

Jeff's apartment is obviously constructed and filmed as a *theatrical set with four sides,* if the reader will permit this paradox. The structure of its space lends itself quite strongly to this impression: The room is often shown with its widest dimension coinciding with the width of the screen image and has doorways on either side that open onto rooms we do not enter.[7] To this setup the forced immobility of James Stewart adds a new touch of theatrical constraint. Let us not forget that *Rear Window* comes immediately after *Dial "M" for Murder* (also with Grace Kelly) and a few years after *Rope,* which was a practice session in Hitchcock's investigation of filmed theater.

Let us push the idea to absurdity and imagine a theatrical version of *Rear Window:* In it the characters would face toward us, and we wouldn't see the courtyard – it would exist for us through sound, and through the remarks and reactions of the characters in the apartment. This rather awkward arrangement is nonetheless to be found in certain moments of theater when the actors, looking out over the audience, see and comment on an enormous space (of a battle, a ceremony, etc.), thus creating a sort of imaginary cone that extends out to infinity from its point of origin on the stage.

In *Rear Window,* the conjuring away of the fourth side – which is *on all sides* of James Stewart's apartment – would serve to facilitate the strange and magical grafting of a theatrical apartment onto a courtyard of the cinema.

Originally published as *"Rear Window* d'Alfred Hitchcock: Le Quatrième coté," in *Cahiers du Cinéma,* No. 356 (February 1984), 4–7. Translated by Jane Belton and Alan Williams. Reprinted with the permission of the author.

NOTES

1. Chion's word is *cour* – the film's title in French is *Fenêtre sur cour,* or "Window on the Courtyard." But while in a European context the nearest analogue would be a single courtyard of a large apartment complex, Hitchcock's New York set represents a number of individual back yards attached to distinct, architecturally different buildings on a single city block. The word *cour* is translated in different ways here, depending on Chion's use of it and on American viewers' understanding of the fictional space. [A.W.]
2. Jeff's kitchen has no door; it is situated in an alcove behind a wall-like bookcase containing books, exotic artifacts, and photographs. There appears to be a bathroom on the other side of the apartment; this is where Lisa retreats to change into her nightgown when she stays overnight. It is not clear whether there is a separate bedroom. Jeff appears to sleep in his living room. In other words, this is a one-room studio apartment.
3. François Truffaut, *Truffaut/Hitchcock* (New York: Simon and Schuster, 1967), 162.
4. Oudart, "La Suture" (*Cahiers du Cinéma,* Nos. 211 and 212), trans. Kari Hanet in Nick Browne, ed., *Cahiers du Cinéma, 1969–1972: The Politics of Representation* (Cambridge, MA: Harvard University Press, 1990), 45–57. For Oudart, the cinema (like *Rear Window* here) depends upon the repression of a fourth side or absent field, upon a process of posing, then filling in absences. It is this process that constitutes the spectator as a subject in cinematic discourse, that engages the spectator in the construction of cinematic space. In this sense, it could be said that *Rear Window* implicitly acknowledges this absent field and explores the way the spectator is involved in the construction of cinematic space and in the stitching together of a narrative. [Ed.]

5. Like the optical point of view that is centered in Jeff's apartment, there is an aural point of view that similarly extends outward into the courtyard. Of course, the central characters talk within Jeff's apartment and, once or twice, we hear the sound of Jeff's door open and close as guests enter or leave. But we *never* hear any sounds from the neighbors who live above, below, or on either side of Jeff's apartment. This aural point of view relies upon a repression similar to that of the fourth side. This repression functions to direct our attention outward into the courtyard. This is violated, only once, at the end of the film when we hear Thorwald's footsteps thumping up Jeff's stairway and the sounds of Thorwald unscrewing lights in the hallway outside Jeff's door. [Ed.]

6. In *First Name: Carmen,* Godard arbitrarily starts and stops the sound effects of the sea (which, by the way, do not accompany images of the sea but rather those of the city). Similarly, Hitchcock subjectively manipulates the flow of sound effects and their sound levels, seemingly starting and stopping them at will. [Ed.]

7. In French, the right and left sides of a stage set are called the *coté cour* and the *coté jardin;* Chion uses these terms to make a pun, which is not translatable from French and has been omitted here. [A.W.]

5 Eternal Vigilance in *Rear Window*

The price of democracy is eternal vigilance.
(William T. Lhaman, *Deliberate Speed*)[1]

One disconcerting aspect of Hollywood's film-making system is the illusory distance it offers from contemporary politics; the manufacture of escapist entertainment isolates fantasy from its origins in real-life anxiety. Alfred Hitchcock's success as a Hollywood film maker comes from making exciting the subliminal connection between fantasy and reality. He is widely thought to divert audiences with fictions of vicarious experiences and is hardly appreciated for gauging the social/moral temper of his times (although his most popular films are credited with influencing the intellectual atmosphere). Social themes do appear in Hitchcock's movies, but the overt political intrigue in *The Man Who Knew Too Much* (1934, 1956) or *Notorious* (1946) or *The Wrong Man* (1956) or *Torn Curtain* (1966), while leading scholars to analyze fascinating psychological subtext, still cloaks the very important political meaning that lies beneath the surface of his work and that becomes more clearly visible in the films of the subsequent generation of film makers Hitchcock inspired.

"Did you kill him because he liked you? Just because he liked you?" screams an outraged neighbor after her pet's death, a murder no one owns up to in *Rear Window*. This key moment cuts to the heart of everyday American politics. It is, most importantly, a stunning accusation of the alienation of postwar society. Witnessing it, the film's protagonist L. B. Jefferies (James Stewart), a photojournalist recuperating from a broken leg, and his fiancée Lisa (Grace Kelly) drop their insouciant banter and turn rigid with shame. It's this sort of unnerving social outburst, keyed to the narrative strain in *Rear Window,* that accounts for the film's prevailing influence on subsequent film culture.

Hitchcock's films have tended to be seen as apolitical, as transcendent masterpieces, as "pure cinema."[2] Indeed, if a film like *Rear Window* is compared to the "remakes" that were inspired by it – films such as *Blow-Up, The Conversation,* and *Blow Out,* the remakes initially strike one as more political. Antonioni focuses on social alienation in contemporary London; Coppola's film about eavesdropping emerges as a commentary on Watergate; and De Palma's movie recalls the scandal of Chappaquiddick, the Kennedy assassinations, and conspiracy theories of CIA coverups. But *Rear Window* has an influence on these films that goes beyond basic plot concepts and formal techniques.

In addition to its thematic investigation of sex, violence, and marriage, *Rear Window*'s tale is a social study, relevant to issues of individual survival in the modern world – to how citizens cope with the difficult or dehumanizing structures of social life. Hitchcock's social vision – rarely discussed by scholars – lies at the very center of *Rear Window,* and it is this vision that directors such as Michelangelo Antonioni, Brian De Palma, and Francis Ford Coppola understood and acknowledged in their reworkings of the *Rear Window* story.

Hitchcock begins constructing this social vision in the very first few shots of the film which survey the court yard and which evoke the more flexible, improvised style of someone like Jean Renoir. But, as Leo Braudy points out, Hitchcock's use of a generically "closed" film form refashions Renoir's documentary, naturalistic "open" approach. In his comparison of Hitchcock (and Lang) to Renoir, Braudy identifies Hitchcock with the closed film, in which the frame of the screen "totally defines the world inside as a picture frame does," and Renoir with the open film, in which the frame is "more like a window, opening a privileged view on a world of which other views are possible."[3] Thus Hitchcock's window on the world is enclosed within a theatrical space. The film's apparent openness exists in a sly, aesthetic tension with a closedness. This tension starts with *Rear Window*'s first shot – a visual joke – of window blinds rising like theater curtains.

Hitchcock plays with the idea of social revelation, alluding to the exhilarating scene in Renoir's *Le Crime de M. Lange* (1936), where a bedridden young man (also with his leg in a cast) is invited to rejoin the world when his boarded-up window is pried open and the life of the courtyard spills in as the narrative surges outward. The social and political implications of this act are clear: The young man's liberation immediately follows the creation of a workers' collective; the billboard that blocks his window is an advertisement for an unpublished magazine that epitomizes the villain's corrupt capitalistic practices. The raising of the bamboo shades in *Rear Window,* though superficially an act of theater, is profoundly political as well. It not only introduces a social space beyond the private space of the central character's apartment, but it also reveals the basic trajectory of the film, which is to expose and then to explore the tension between private and public, interior and exterior, the individual and the community. Although an (en)closed film, *Rear Window*'s first scene opens out to reveal variety and diversity, to an openness that could be compared to Renoir (or, today, to Altman). Yet the film never commits to complete realism.

Robert Burks's camera pulls in to the courtyard, an obvious set of the back side of several apartment buildings, which represents an alternate view of a tumultuous social scene. It's an exploration of life through its obvious, almost self-conscious mimesis. This artificial realism contests noncontradictory notions of modern perception. Hitchcock experiments with Hollywood's glossy, detailed stylizations while approximating Renoir's varied, shifting views of real life. Such a stylistic and philosophical hybrid influences film makers to this day.

Hitchcock's "closed" courtyard pits neighbor against neighbor: Thorwald (Burr, right) snaps back at the Sculptress (Jesslyn Fax, left) when she volunteers gardening advice. Photo courtesy of Paramount.

What Braudy elsewhere called an "expressionistic attack against the sufficiency of the visual world" also explains post–World War II skepticism and wonder, a paradoxical view also illustrated in such art movements as the Nouvelle Vague, which melded verité techniques with imaginative romanticism. *Rear Window,* a product of the post–World War II Hollywood that was including more evidence of the documentary world and heterogeneous society into its fictions (see Kazan's *On the Waterfront,* 1954), idealizes the modernist exercises of self-conscious form and political reality and imaginative fiction.[4] They play off each other, even in Franz Waxman's sound-of-New York score which is also an artifice – a musical impression of urban energy that contributes to the tension between reality and perception, fiction, and politics. It fires up rather than settles the audience's self-consciousness. The backyard and terraced set design, featuring a slivered view of street traffic, works similarly. It is both closed and open, contained yet suggesting the uncontainable. In modernist fashion it recalls both William Wyler's *Dead End* (1937) stage set and the psychological projection of street life in Busby Berkeley's "Lullaby of Broadway" production number in *The Golddiggers of 1935* (1935). (*Rear Window*'s celebration of movieness resonates in later films: Hitchcock's in/out/in window pirouette prefigures Antonioni's defenestrating camera at the end of *The Passenger,* 1975; Burks's settling on a bead of sweat trailing down Stewart's forehead anticipates the hot summer, New York village/ghetto survey that begins Spike Lee's *Do the Right Thing,* 1989.)

Understood today, Hitchcock's artifice makes unexpected use of Hollywood tropes, relating them to the artistic aspirations of the 1950s zeitgeist. In William T. Lhamon, Jr.'s, *Deliberate Speed,* a study of the aesthetic and political advances generally overlooked in 1950s culture and society, mainstream movies are neglected. But Lhamon's thesis fits the inadvertent institutional subversions of some Hollywood professional products, particularly *Rear Window:*

> As the price of democracy is eternal vigilance, so the cost of vital culture is its continual re-creation. People never find out who they are, or their value, by looking into someone else's mirror, nor by accepting cultural judgments from an earlier time. Those reflections are necessary correctives. They guide people toward goals and around pitfalls. But a living culture constantly adapts the usable past to present pressures. Not the other way around. When critics measure the present only with past yardsticks, or when they fail to search widely enough for an era's authentic gestures, then it appears to them that no usable present culture exists.[5]

By making each window that L. B. Jefferies spies on a little movie in itself, by referring audiences to the artificiality of the storytelling they behold, Hitchcock builds upon the movies' cultural history and *adapts the usable past to present pressures.* As Jefferies measures his own stultified life against those of his observable neighbors, Hitchcock's audience is also able to gauge the progress, health, and safety of their lives by this thriller. Other film makers have demonstrated Lhamon's prescription by looking into Hitchcock's mirror not as an end in itself but to find ways of explaining their own eras and experiences to themselves – Brian De Palma is chief among these culturally aware, rigorous artists. Voyeurism, an abiding De Palma theme, got perhaps its first full Hollywood treatment in *Rear Window,* but De Palma was able to expand its implications in several films just as Michelangelo Antonioni revised Hitchcock's investigatory premise in *Blow Up* (1966) and Francis Coppola adopted both Hitchcock's and Antonioni's studies of social vigilance in *The Conversation* (1974).

"We've become a race of peeping Toms," exclaims Stella (Thelma Ritter) to Jefferies, suggesting the 1950s era's caution about the explosion of technology and bombs, of global curiosity and interference. *Rear Window*'s forgotten social context (it was made during the Korean conflict and the Rosenberg trial) makes Stella's alarm resonant. Although it has become the convention to read Hitchcock apolitically, doing so limits *Rear Window*'s meanings as well as its significance to film makers working in more socially conscious periods, or at least openly concerned with the problems of political activity and social engagement. From *Rear Window* on, film artists had a model for exploring the psychic costs of the newly felt need for eternal vigilance.

Rear Window's title suggests a backyard view, secrets revealed through peeking, peeping. Hitchcock's post–World War II uncovering of average American loneliness, deception, mundanity, and horror has become a formalized example of cinematic investigation and social transgression. Its effect on later film makers is as notable for the technical standardization of multiple viewpoints, and the mechanical manipulation of sound and image into the arsenal of cinematic espionage, as it is for establishing – and legitimizing – a generic form of sociological skepticism. The public accusation, "Why did you kill him?" resounds throughout Hitchcock's oeuvre and the post-bomb world.

While Antonioni's *Blow Up* suggests an homage to *Rear Window* through its photographer protagonist's accidentally witnessing a murder then utilizing the apparatus of image making to confirm and reveal the deed – uncovering the truth – it operates in a field of art cinema that Hitchcock never pretended to. *Rear Window* uses the narrative forms of popular movie making to effect a nearly subversive viewer-consciousness. This is part of its focus on average American social locations and the class diversity of its characters. Hitchcock's method of bringing terror close (as dramatized in the climactic, agonizing, life-or-death fight scene) functions in the pop-art mode of making the profound ordinary. Antonioni's extraordinary approach to showing human experience through the habits and effluvia of modernity itself adapted Hitchcock's usable past art work to his own meanings: Jefferies's prone position symbolizes the halting emotional state of most Antonioni protagonists. *Blow Up* thus created a generic offshoot that includes Coppola's *The Conversation* and De Palma's *Blow Out* (1981). These modernist investigations of both cinema and the ineffable differ significantly from *Rear Window* by virtue of their constant, explicit apprehensiveness. Hitchcock posits, in the American quotidian, a presumed sense of justice – even after World War II progressivism mandated a need for social change – that implies, at least superficially, some basic social certainties (marriage, authority). *Rear Window*'s elements of spying and snooping probe the postwar experience of American rejuvenation and political tumult even as its mainstream Hollywood form, as such, countermands change for the comfort implicit in classical style, narrative cohesion, and the exercise of shock and suspense. Still, the latter, open-ended ideas would be used extensively in later film eras.

Hitchcock's romantic (Hollywood) psychology tends to distract from a sociological reading. The impotence theme – Stella's comment that "those bathing beauties you've been watching haven't raised your temperature one degree in a month" – obviously pinpoints Jefferies's deepest fear (of intimacy). And many details fit this conventional reading: A shot of Thorwald (Raymond Burr) returning from the garden leads to a shot of the Newlyweds with

An Image of Urban Alienation: Miss Lonely Hearts (Judith Evelyn) entertains an imaginary guest for dinner. Photo courtesy of Paramount.

"That's Amore" heard on calliope; there is, as well, the Miss Lonely Hearts subplot where an aspect of Nathaniel West's dire urban misery is averted (a suicide attempt interrupted, dissuaded by music). But though these legitimate Hollywood themes, left in a romantic-mystery context, could become banal, *Rear Window* more interestingly leans toward the film noir movement by its clever, post–World War II insistence on social dread. (Jefferies and his police detective pal, Doyle, are both war vets whose resignation makes them suspicious and wary citizens.) The particular urban American quality of this dread is set out in Jefferies's expressed difficulty (and subtle antagonism) with Lisa, his socialite fiancée. Lisa's argument about social place ("I can't fit in here – you can't fit in there") dramatizes cultural differences and points to the problem of social-sympathy that recurs in several of Stella's quips, such as her final line: "No thanks – I don't want any part of it!" This line makes a joke of urban alienation while, at the same time, mocking human curiosity.[6] *Rear Window* mocks the suspense genre's social complacency by invoking a series of pantomimed neighborhood terrors and cruelties, such as Miss Lonely Hearts's near-rape and suicidal despondency. By loading the suspense genre with postwar fright, Hitchcock brings social adversity to the fore of pop consciousness.

De Palma's reworking of *Rear Window* in *Sisters* (1973) sees through Jefferies's game of detection and responds intuitively to Hitchcock's enriching humanism, thus expanding on Hitchcock's approach to the suspense genre. In *Sisters,* a female reporter, Grace Collier (Jennifer Salt), takes on the role of Hitchcock's male photojournalist, Jefferies: She witnesses a murder in an apartment across the way and spends the remainder of the film attempting to prove to authorities that the crime actually took place. Despite its sense of theatrical (psychological) closure, *Rear Window* is essentially an urban vision, whereas *Sisters* flips social vision into a psychological tale. Having ingested the earlier ordeal of Antonioni's photographer in *Blow Up,* who just happens to shoot a murder – and, in the process, discovering his own impotence and powerlessness – De Palma pinpoints the particular dread of his own era.[7] De Palma had taken a humorous approach to *Blow Up* in *Greetings* (1968), in which an assassination conspiracy buff hung up on the Zapruder film of the JFK killing dates a woman who dashes his mania by referring to Antonioni's treatment of perception and detection. Thus *Greetings* maintains the late-1960s reality of political obsession. This suggests that Hollywood generic convention is no longer believed in as such (signs of a faithless culture). Genre presumptions had to change after such harsh intrusions as urban unrest and political distrust – the salient points of De Palma's early, counterculture comedies *Greetings* and *Hi, Mom!* (1970).

Following *Rear Window*'s example, other film makers found it necessary themselves to reconsider the world as a dystopia to be spied on and examined. Antonioni, Coppola, and De Palma of *Blow Out* do this by investigating specialized worlds – that of the leisured class and of the educated and professional classes. But it is De Palma's *Sisters* that revisits *Rear Window*'s democratic, working-

De Palma's *Rear Window:* In *Sisters*, female reporter Grace Collier (Jennifer Salt) becomes a refiguration of Hitchcock's voyeuristic male photojournalist. Photo courtesy of American International.

class environs to make the earlier film's interest in social exploration clearer and more pertinent. The Staten Island setting marked *Sisters* as a film about class. At the same time, De Palma addresses issues of race and miscegenation as well as making his own impudent acknowledgment of feminism. He tackles a new, 1970s social reality that alters *Rear Window*'s 1950s generic tropes. In *Hi, Mom!*, De Palma already parodied the pop era's use of television, media consciousness, and radical politics, pushing *Rear Window*'s sense of cultural trepidation even farther.

Much of *Sisters'* action is a tease. Like the birthday-cake-and-butcher-knife held aloft, the film is a grand guignol joke. De Palma develops a different, sophomoric, *pop* brand of humor that differs from Hitchcock's ominous wit. He realizes that, by 1973,

Hitchcockian suspense is well known, almost a camp device, and references to it emerge as a film generation spoof.[8] There's no way to refer to Hitchcock's style without kidding it some, and this kidding needs to be understood as central to De Palma's contemporary sensibility, not as a lack of sophistication or a crude imitation of exactly what Hitchcock was doing. In *Sisters*, the use of the TV frame establishes a self-consciousness about watching, about the media and its reframed reality. This is because *Rear Window*'s boldest unofficial sequel was, in fact, the Zapruder film which added existential shock to Hitchcock's classic myth of dangerous vigilance. (*Rear Window*, in which each apartment across the way is like a TV screen, presaged TV viewing the way the peep-art film making in *Hi, Mom!* presaged video camcorders.) *Sisters* opens with a TV game show called "Peeping Toms." The game's winner is a black man (Lisle Wilson) whose race is pandered to with a prize, dinner for two at the "African Room."

De Palma extends his voyeur theme with Emil (William Finley), who watches Danielle Blanchion (Margot Kidder) from many vantage points – from the street, from his car, and, significantly, from the TV studio audience. All this jokiness, done while playing out a bloody, brutal scenario, is less suggestive of *Rear Window* than of post-*Psycho*, post-Zapruder absurdism.

Rear Window's classical Hollywood stylistic and narrative tropes – the luxe photography, the A-list star casting – has passed through the culture to have a more benign emotional effect. Yet De Palma insists on the potency of his ideas, the unexpected brute force of its content, such as the shocking final confrontation between Jefferies and Thorwald. It was in *Psycho* that Hitchcock changed the mainstream cinema's regard of terror – the possibility of terror in the world outside the theater became part of the film language that could menace the in-theater audience's fantasizing. Hitchcock's move into modernism and existential angst vastly influenced De Palma's generation through its expression of modern despair.

Sisters inherits this despair legitimately, but De Palma's originality comes in the way he connects an aesthetic advance to revolu-

De Palma's *Rear Window:* In *Sisters*, the murder is witnessed by Grace and seen in a split screen, which combines her point-of-view shot and a reverse shot. Photo courtesy of American International.

tionary political content – the heroine Grace Collier's social skepticism about the police, race, and feminism. A reporter for her hometown Staten Island newspaper, she writes investigative journalism; she is a child of the student-protest era that figured so largely in De Palma's first three movies. (Displayed on her apartment wall is her own press clipping with the headline "Why We Call Them Pigs.") Grace dares to invoke the police department's racism: "White woman kills her black lover and the police don't care anything about it!" "These people are always stabbing each other," says one of the cops visiting the crime scene. In *Rear Window,* Jefferies playfully satirizes police mentality when talking with his old friend, police detective Doyle, but he clearly recognizes and supports the authority of the law. Grace threatens to expose the corruption and indifference of the police with a newspaper story that "police refuse to investigate brutal race murder." She warns, "this isn't a police state yet," a line as accusatory as the 1950s line from *Rear Window* cited earlier: "Did you kill him because he liked you?" This political material is often downplayed in De Palma's work by critics (and viewers) not conversant with his origins in the social-political-artistic ferment in the 1960s, but it is an important part of his different aesthetic modernism – his evolution from Hitchcock (where the only black character in *Rear Window* is a babysitter's disembodied voice on the telephone) to a story in which race plays a central role.

De Palma's own radicalism shows in his continuation of Andy Warhol's *Chelsea Girls* (1966) split-screen experiment – a technique De Palma first essayed in *Dionysus in '69* (1970), a transcription that sought to turn live theater into the material of cinema. *Sisters* develops the experiment as both an efficient narrative device and a demonstration of divided consciousness. The simultaneity of events as shown (we see the murder from Grace's POV on one half of the screen, and we see her watching it on another), split into opposing halves of the screen, objectifies watching – much as the multiple apartments on view in *Rear Window* turned urban architecture into the material of cinema, or at least of theater. Hitchcock's set design applies almost a sociological grid to various urban social styles – an animated diagram that facilitates Jefferies's and our observation and contemplation. *Sisters* breaks the grid apart as De Palma exploits scopophilia's third dimension; its effect is to penetrate the sequestered lives of individual apartment dwellers: showing all sides and rooms of Danielle's habitat, implicitly stretching Grace's vision across the space separating her from her neighbors. By this method De Palma's audiences are made to hold opposing thoughts (two spaces, two actions, two protagonists) in the mind (and on the screen) at one time. Tension (recognized in superficial narrative terms as "suspense") results, but there is, more significantly, an expression of doubled consciousness, opposed social, political, and spiritual views: Grace the American woman versus Danielle the immigrant woman; Grace the social radical versus Danielle the conservative assimilator; Grace a figure of social dissent (derived, in part, from Jennifer Salt's role in *Hi, Mom!*) versus Danielle, apathetic in true post-1960s style. De Palma is working out a thesis on the danger inherent in these separate, enclosed social roles (a theme that is repeated in *Blow Out* and *Casualties of War*, 1989). The compulsion to act on distressing knowledge (Grace's unrest) counters nonsocial behavior (Danielle's surface docility). Yet Danielle's psychological split imputes peril to 1970s social complacency. Her lack of consciousness – her strict opposition of social and antisocial being as characterized by her alter ego Siamese twin Dominique – proves malevolent. *Sisters* adds political consequence to the dilemmas of *Rear Window*'s characters. The musical score accompanying all this is crucial. De Palma's commissioning of Bernard Herrmann's anxious strings and throbbing horns carries Hitchcock's aesthetic forward into modern emotional atonality.[9]

De Palma also intensifies this metacinematic approach: Grace watches and leaps in where Jefferies was slowly drawn into trouble and mystery. With binoculars, Grace spies on a detective (Charles Durning) in the apartment across the way in real time much as Jefferies watched Lisa as she trespassed on private territory, looking for evidence, courting danger. But in transposing *Rear Window*'s tale, De Palma bifurcates the hero into watcher and watched. This follows a shift in art and social awareness that speaks to the history of cinematic discourse and subscribes to modernism's existential unknowing. Grace takes over Danielle's tale just as De Palma's social ambivalence replaces Hitchcock's implicit sponsoring of the Jefferies character. (The walls of Grace's apartment feature a timely collage – abstract modern art and news clippings.) A 1970s, New Hollywood ethic held that storytelling wasn't enough; it must be connected to some social engagement – which De Palma is not ashamed to assert, even in *Sisters'* comic slasher-film atmosphere.

Politics change things – queering comfortable, traditional ideas of cinema's (entertainment's) function as well as disturbing a usual sense of justice and stability. A comic pratfall with a cake (Grace slips on the recently mopped floor, destroying evidence of the murder) lets De Palma parody modern absurdity. Controlling dramatic logic, his plot goes crazy – just like the world.

The man who mopped the floor, Emil Breton (an art parody/relative of Andre Breton?), indicates the deliberate, game-playing use of visual tricks and media forms that De Palma employs. Art consciousness, suppressed by a classically styled film maker like Hitchcock, is one of the features that distinguishes De Palma's work. As for De Palma's homages to Hitchcock, it's bad scholarship to assume that he merely imitates or steals from Hitchcock. One must first recognize his prerogative, possibly exercised here with Breton, to quote preexisting art and art-ideas. Most of all, De Palma represents a contemporary reassessment of the ideas in Hitchcock's work – a rethought philosophy similar to surrealism's response to the Romantic movement. Befitting cinema as a kinetic medium, this complication includes mixing points of view within a single narrative – literalized in the split screen effect – a change as major as cubism's response to representational realism.

These changes prepare for the confusion of viewpoints when Grace visits a newsmagazine and is shown a TV-style documentary on the Blanchion twins. Complexity occurs mostly in the asylum sequence following it where, under sedation, Grace's nightmare becomes a combination of hysteria and real-life fear such as is exhibited in the Salvador Dali dream sequence in Hitchcock's *Spellbound* (1945). Following surrealist logic, in the nightmare Grace's subconscious takes visible form. Yet in *Sisters* (unlike in *Spellbound*), De Palma depicts the subconscious in modern, media-savvy ways. Grace's fear of experience gets its tone from the horror she felt seeing the documentary of the Blanchion Siamese twins' separation. Here, De Palma has grisly fun with the notion of splitting and fusion. He conjoins Grace to her nemesis Danielle the same way this sequence fuses the wide-angle lens of mock-documentary film making with the obvious scare tactics of exploitation movies. *Sisters* absorbs more than Hitchcock's influence in these points (though it is important to remember Hitchcock's own borrowing of exploitation tropes in *Psycho*). De Palma goes from videotapes of the Blanchion twins back to TV framing – "real-life horror" featuring an appearance by Pierre Milius (a cameo appearance by De Palma's New Hollywood colleague, writer/director John Milius), a doctor whose presence satirizes magisterial *auteur*ism. When Emil commences the appalling surgery that spooks Grace, he is seen as Caligari-like and so is shot with a distorting fisheye lens. (Movie maven De Palma evokes John Frankenheimer's *Seconds* [1966], having already satirized *The Cabinet of Dr. Caligari* [1919] in his 1964 short, *Wotan's Wake*.)

An even greater cultural shift is seen in Grace's rounded, iris-framed vision, conveying both her temporary split identity and her memory. Based on black-and-white video imagery, Grace's imagined fright includes being observed ("they're gonna hurt me!"). It's a tour-de-force scene that pushes Grace's half-conscious/half-drugged state to a degree that Hitchcock would not have dared because it was not consonant with popular, post–World War II notions of vision and experience. De Palma's approach has a particular relevance to contemporary vision and experience – it resembles an LSD trip. Thus, it references a new generation's sense of altered reality and paranoia through drug culture, the ultimate retreat from social responsibility.

Playing out this new trepidation, in this sequence Danielle's dominating id, Dominique, latches onto the rational Grace – irrational forces exerting their dominance via Dominique. It's just nature's cruelty, evident in the biological mutation exemplified by the Siamese twins. Fate – a Hitchcock preoccupation – is manifested frighteningly through images of chaos and absurdity (tap-dancing Siamese twins) that veer into parodic savagery in synch with the modern (1970s) sense of the outré.

Like Hitchcock, De Palma's notion of human experience is expressed in metaphors of seeing. Protagonists search, look, and observe, seeking to know yet finding themselves, at the risk-filled moment of revelation, to be helpless. Movie watching is the function that Hitchcock played with and that the impudent De Palma analyzes. At this point in *Sisters*, Sam Fuller's *Shock Corridor* (1963) with its combination of Sartrean *No Exit* existential angst (through a mistaken-identity plot development) crowds out *Rear Window*. Repressed knowledge seems more terrifying, deeper than Fuller's hatred for political tyranny. "We'll share our secrets," Emil tells Grace, then, switching to Danielle, says, "Every time I made love to you Dominique came back." His killing – following the first motif of knife slashes at male sex organs – dramatizes female stress and defense. Grace shares this when her hands drip male genital blood. This too is Hitchcockian, a suggestion of the subterranean impulses governing behavior. No more a fetishist of female victimization than was Hitchcock, De Palma details the intimate nature of female distress. When Grace asks a neurotic patient named Arlene for permission to use a pay phone, they make eye contact. This contact is an indication of future "madness" and of women's shared sociopolitical plight, and is similar to the eye contact made between Kate (Angie Dickinson) and Liz (Nancy Allen) in *Dressed to Kill* (1980). These women are sisters in madness, in torment. By the 1970s, American society similarly came face to face with its destructive, divided natures, a confrontation like Jefferies's and Thorwald's that in the 1950s Hitchcock could only suggest and had to keep in the dark.

When *Sisters'* plot tension is temporarily resolved and Grace is back in the bedroom of her adolescence in her mother's home, another kind of entrapment is apparent. There's a Beatles poster, a Fabian photo, a Raggedy Ann doll – escapist pop art on the walls. This is De Palma's modern truth – personal withdrawal with clearly political implications. It looks back to Jefferies's behavior in *Rear Window* – to his withdrawal from social responsibility (marriage to Lisa) and his escape into the fantasies he constructs about his neighbors.

Francis Coppola's own obsession with technology as a dubious sinecure from social trouble updates both Hitchcock's underappreciated aestheticism and Antonioni's alienated yet politicized transposition of the *Rear Window* idea to the mod scene of 1960s London in *Blow Up*. They merge in *The Conversation*'s reconstitution of Hitchcock's urban thriller and Antonioni's existential suspense story. Where the latter can be seen to distill Hitchcock's pantomimes of the commonplace (the actions of the neighbors) into a bourgeois tennis game, Coppola fashions a paranoid fantasia on the themes of spying and social unease, uncannily coincident with the political revelations of the 1972 Watergate scandal.

Coppola's *Rear Window:* Harry Caul (Gene Hackman, left) eavesdrops on a young couple in the park in *The Conversation.* Hitchcock's pantomimed action across the courtyard is transformed into literal mimes who appear in both *Blow Up* and *The Conversation.* Photo courtesy of Paramount.

Democracy's eternal vigilance is here turned upside down; spying is no longer a form of vigilance but rather a cause for trepidation.

Coppola's protagonist, Harry Caul (Gene Hackman), matches L. B. Jefferies fear for fear, ultimately rivaling his psychological vulnerability. Though culpable in terms of social corruption, Caul, like Grace Collier, discovers his own form of paralysis, his inability to act or to change the dire circumstances he uncovers. Caul and Grace differ from Hitchcock's more innocent characters, although they indubitably derive from them: These 1970s protagonists evince a tragic naiveté. Advanced technology does not help them; neither does increased social cynicism. (The latter helps contemporary audiences relate to them just as 1950s audiences did to Jefferies's good-hearted seclusion.) The crosshairs of the surveillance microphone used by Caul's team of eavesdroppers target the directional viewpoints (and audio points) that were random in *Rear Window* to get a closer, more focused view of things. However, this is not more revealing; it is, instead, more isolated and creepier. Jefferies's shut-in stasis is made into a profession (Caul's professional eavesdropper), made cultural, a miasma. (In this, Coppola's technology also looks ahead: Its perched telescope anticipates the spy apparatus in Godard's *Detective* [1985]; the tape recorder dials – shown when Caul reconstructs the park conversion he bugged – augur De Palma's fetishizing close-ups of sound-recording technology in *Blow Out*'s detection scenes.)

It's no coincidence that *The Conversation*'s opening surveillance sequence resembles the sighting of assassination targets; the terror of 1960s political murders lays the foundation for the paranoid atmosphere Coppola constructs. This detail is as socially conscious as it is art (movie) conscious.[10] *The Conversation* is not realistic like the French noir whose tone it resembles, Bertrand Tavernier's *The Clockmaker* (1973). Within the ominous quiet of Caul's calculation and suspicion, Coppola adds elements of absurdism and 1970s paranoia – a hyperintensity where small objects, unexpected gestures by strangers gain mysterious effect. Hitchcock's superdetailed, artificial naturalism in *Rear Window* suggested this, too, although it took the revolution of the Nouvelle Vague and the 1960s American Independent movement (e.g., Cassavetes) to normalize the delicate shift between stylization and verité that with Coppola's aplomb registers as normal. (In Caul's workshop, amidst his electronic equipment, nature appears as an artificial forest of fake palm trees – a literary precursor of this exact oddity can be found in Norman Mailer's 1964 pop novel, *An American Dream*.)

Coppola's self-reflexivity works in line with Hitchcock's cinema tricks. Those flashbulb burnouts that briefly staved off Thorwald's attack on Jefferies were also devices of sophisticated narrativity; their equivalent in *The Conversation* is seen in Coppola's many replays of its central recorded moment: The telephoto rack focus is shown so that sharpening the recalled image matches the increased clarity of the conversation's sound.

As much as De Palma partakes of a changed Hollywood's

license for film makers' political expression, Coppola, too, uses technological aptitude for emotional revelation. The theme of eternal vigilance matches his concern with the appropriateness of cinematic knowledge and technological prowess. Caul's involvement with a case after his willed detachment demonstrates his sense of obligation and unavoidable responsibility. His emotionally handicapped, high-tech world holds no protection. Blamelessness, the bogey of pre–World War II isolationism and post-Vietnam apathy, is impossible. After callously invading strangers' privacy, Caul's conscience is haunted; his shrinking world is suffused with guilt. The shame Hitchcock pointed at after the killing of a neighbor's dog is, twenty years later, a national epidemic.

Whenever Caul poignantly remembers the dangerous conversation he has on tape, he experiences a longing for romance and connection – the very desires that Jefferies and Collier feared. What once seemed socially impractical is dramatized as personal incapacity; each protagonist faces danger through the void in themselves, by a failure to connect (symbolized by Jefferies's strangely disconnected, sleep-filled, "marital" bliss at the end, by Grace's wiped-out memory, by Caul's stripped-down apartment).

Hitchcock's supreme visual-aural manipulation has its legacy in the way Coppola sets forth Caul's memory – although a sound recordist, he puts clues together visually (as sound recorder Jack Terry [John Travolta] does in *Blow Out*). Indicating the primacy of the visual image thusly, Coppola posits film as memory and memory as a moral adjunct to gaining knowledge. Film and vision are both shown to be crucial physical acts and fearsome, if natural, moral actions or social duties.

De Palma's *Blow Out* is a significant exposition of cinema's effect as a sociological analog. Jack Terry's uncertainty and apathy relate to 1980s spiritual trauma that fits Braudy's description of Hitchcock's interest in ambiguity and the pursuit of knowledge.

[Fritz] Lang and Hitchcock imply that . . . ambiguity is a reason to look beyond the surface of things because for them the visual world is filled with deception. Hitchcock's interest in voyeurism is the perfect mirror to Lang's interest in blindness; both constitute a post-Christian attack on the truth of surfaces in which the invisible cosmic order has been identified with individual sexual and psychological darkness. By degrees Hitchcock implicates first his characters . . . and finally his audience as well . . . in the act of irresponsible seeing we call voyeurism.[11]

Blow Out demonstrates in grand, almost operatic terms of cinema extravagance (its play with deep focus, camera movement, hearing and seeing, eavesdropping, and obsession) the way contemporary artists build upon *Rear Window*'s insights. De Palma does not acquiesce to Hollywood convention; that would be a mere imitation of dramatic effect that Braudy praised Lang and Hitchcock for avoiding. Instead, De Palma attaches topical experience and the political lore of assassinations and coverups to Hitchcock's paradigm.

De Palma's virtuoso mise-en-scène refers much to Hitchcock's emphasis on visual information and cinematic manipulation. (In *Body Double* [1984], the plot repeats certain *Rear Window* motifs, but its style more often quotes the lavishly kinetic *Vertigo* [1958].) And *Rear Window*'s aesthetic impact was felt beyond De Palma. John Huston's *Reflections in a Golden Eye* (1967) also contains Hitchcock's ideas on voyeurism and secret lives. Huston uses an enhanced lighting scheme that recalls the chromatics Robert Burks achieved for Hitchcock's 1950s color films. It lends a quiet tone and manipulative control that brings Hitchcock's interest in human foible and perversity to Carson McCullers's tale of murder and sexual aberration. One of the most extraordinary camera movements in Huston's career is the very Hitchcockian swish pan to each significant character involved in the film's tragic climax. (It anticipates the slow plan across the destroyed domestic space at the end of Francis Coppola's *The Conversation* as well as the three-focal-point swish pan that De Palma used in the footchase sequence of *The Fury*, 1978.) It is Hitchcock's audacity that is seen in these other American film makers' free, self-conscious, dramatic use of camera position and function to illustrate the emotional vectors of a scene.

In the postwar (World War II, Vietnam) experience, moral expedience is a profound preoccupation. It unsettles the exercise of genre, evidenced in Hitchcock's complex exposition of *Rear Window*'s simple narrative. That Hitchcock's film has magnetized the imaginations of artists as distinctive as De Palma, Antonioni, Coppola, and others (Michael Powell in *Peeping Tom*, 1960; Jonathan Demme in *The Silence of the Lambs*, 1991; Alan Pakula in *Klute*, 1971; and even Jacques Tati in *Play Time*, 1967) proves its effectiveness as a new myth pare excellence. Its pageant of looking and acting penetrates to deep meanings of community and personal responsibility.

These subsequent movies justly fulfill a vision – that of a world gone mad – scarily hinted at in the glossy deluxe Hollywood splendor of Hitchcock's style in *Rear Window*. To young persons haunted by the line, "did you kill him because he liked you?" the convulsive politics of their own adult years could seem like déja vu – the treachery and insensitivity and pain and doubt already glimpsed across the courtyard by Jefferies via Hitchcock. A later generation that appreciates *The Simpsons'* derision (see note 8) may laugh, but before Bart such movies as *Blow Up*; *Reflections in a Golden Eye*; *Greetings*; *Hi, Mom!*; *Sisters*; *The Conversation*; *Blow Out*; and *Body Double* were confirmations of the seriousness in the fantasy Hitchcock wove. One final difference between these films and *Rear Window* is that Jefferies never photographs what goes on, but many of his progeny do, in some way, make a record of their vigilance. This is plainly due to the change in cultural habit. A faithless age needs the evidence. Disbelief inspires documentation – Hitchcock could have no better tribute to the persuasiveness of *Rear Window*'s sociological lesson.

NOTES

1. William T. Lhaman, Jr., *Deliberate Speed: The Origins of a Cultural Style in the American 1950s* (Washington, DC: Smithsonian Institute Press, 1990), 2.
2. Major studies of the director by Robin Wood, Francois Truffaut, and Donald Spoto treat Hitchcock as transcendent artist. See *Hitchcock's Films*, 3rd ed. (New York: A. S. Barnes, 1977); *Hitchcock*, rev. ed.

(New York: Simon and Schuster, 1984); and *The Art of Alfred Hitchcock* (New York: Hopkinson and Blake, 1976), respectively. It is only recently that critics have begun to investigate the political implications of Hitchcock's cinema. See, for example, Robert J. Corber's *In the Name of National Security: Hitchcock, Homophobia, and the Political Construction of Gender in Postwar America* (Durham, NC: Duke University Press, 1993). Corber suggests that the film's hero, in spying on his neighbors with high-powered lenses, appropriates the apparatus of the national security state and engages in a McCarthyite investigation of sorts. The film's criticism of its hero's voyeuristic practices serves as a "critique of McCarthyism."

3. Leo Braudy, *The World in a Frame: What We See in Films* (New York: Anchor/Doubleday, 1976), 40.
4. Peter Biskind, *Seeing Is Believing: How Hollywood Taught Us to Stop Worrying and Love the Fifties* (New York: Pantheon, 1983).
5. Lhamon, 2.
6. Stella's small but prominent role pays tribute to the otherwise absent perspective of the rank and file and provides an important dimension to Hitchcock's social vision.
7. Years later, Woody Allen's *Manhattan Murder Mystery* (1993) treats this distress comically and thus, unfortunately, makes it trivial.
8. More *Rear Window* influence can be seen in the 1990s TV series *The Simpsons:* Bart breaks his leg while having fun in the pool. During recovery, he looks out his bedroom window and sees his neighbor, Mr. Flanders, burying something (his wife's dead houseplant which he killed by not watering). Bart, feeling Hitchcockian alarm, dials 911 to report a murder to the police. A recorded *Moviephone* voice answers: "You have picked Regicide. If you know the name of the king or queen being killed, press 1 . . ." In another *Simpsons* episode, an apparent murder turns out to be explained by one of Jeff's sarcastic lines from *Rear Window* – "an unemployed magician amusing the neighborhood with his slight of hand."
9. Of course, *Rear Window*'s music was composed by Franz Waxman, not Herrmann. But Herrmann's subsequent association with Hitchcock makes his use by De Palma here an act of homage to Hitchcock.
10. The film's resemblance to Bogdanovich's *Targets* (1968), which was inspired by the sniper Charles Whitman, is subliminal.
11. Braudy, 81.

Filmography

The following films were directed by Alfred Hitchcock:

1926

The Pleasure Garden

Screenplay: Eliot Stannard. Based on the novel by Oliver Sandys

Photography: Baron Ventimiglia

Production: Gainsborough

Ca. 85 mins.

Cast: Virginia Valli, Carmelita Geraghty, Miles Mander, John Stuart

The Mountain Eagle

Screenplay: Eliot Stannard

Photography: Baron Ventimiglia

Production: Gainsborough

Ca. 89 mins.

Cast: Bernard Goetzke, Nita Naldi, Malcolm Keen

The Lodger

Screenplay: Eliot Stannard. Based on the novel by Mrs. Marie
    Adelaide Belloc-Lowndes

Photography: Baron Ventimiglia

Production: Gainsborough

Ca. 100 mins.

Cast: Ivor Novello, June, Malcolm Keen, Marie Ault

1927

Downhill

Screenplay: Eliot Stannard. Based on a play by Ivor Novello and
Constance Collier

Photography: Claude McDonnell

Production: Gainsborough

Ca. 105 mins.

Cast: Ivor Novello, Robin Irvine, Ben Webster, Isabel Jeans, Ian
Hunter

Easy Virtue

Screenplay: Eliot Stannard. Based on a play by Noel Coward

Photography: Claude McDonnell

Production: Gainsborough

Ca. 105 mins.

Cast: Isabel Jeans, Franklin Dyall, Eric Bransby Williams, Ian
Hunter

The Ring

Screenplay: Alfred Hitchcock

Photography: Jack Cox

Production: British International Pictures

Ca. 110 mins.

Cast: Carl Brisson, Lillian Hall-Davies, Ian Hunter, Harry Terry

1928

The Manxman

Screenplay: Eliot Stannard. Based on the novel by Sir
Hall Caine

Photography: Jack Cox

Production: British International Pictures

Ca. 100 mins.

Cast: Carl Brisson, Anny Ondra, Malcolm Keen

The Farmer's Wife

Screenplay: Alfred Hitchcock, Eliot Stannard. Based on a play by
   Eden Philpotts

Photography: Jack Cox

Production: British International Pictures

Ca. 100 mins.

Cast: Lillian Hall-Davies, Jameson Thomas, Maud Gil, Gordon
   Harker

Champagne

Screenplay: Eliot Stannard. Based on a story by Walter C. Mycroft

Photography: Jack Cox

Production: British International Pictures

Ca. 104 mins.

Cast: Betty Balfour, Gordon Harker, Theo von Alten, Jack Trevor

1929

Blackmail

Screenplay: Alfred Hitchcock, Benn W. Levy. Based on a play by
   Charles Bennett

Photography: Jack Cox

Production: British International Pictures

80 mins.

Cast: Anny Ondra (with the voice of Joan Barry), Sara Allgood,
   John Longden, Cyril Ritchard

Juno and the Paycock

Screenplay: Alfred Hitchcock, Alma Reville. Based on the play by
   Sean O'Casey

Photography: Jack Cox

Production: British International Pictures

85 mins.

Cast: Sara Allgood, Edward Chapman, John Laurie, Marie O'Neill

1930

Elstree Calling

Part directed only.

Supervising director: Adrian Brunel

Screenplay: Val Valentine

Photography: Claude Friese-Greene

Production: British International Pictures

7,770 ft.

Cast: Anna May Wang, Donald Calthrop, Gordon Harker

Murder!

Screenplay: Alma Reville, Alfred Hitchcock, Walter Mycroft. Based on the play and novel *Enter Sir John* by Clemence Dane and Helen Simpson

Photography: Jack Cox

Production: British International Pictures

100 mins.

Cast: Herbert Marshall, Norah Baring, Edward Chapman, Phyllis Konstam

1931

The Skin Game

Screenplay: Alma Reville, Alfred Hitchcock. Based on the play by John Galsworthy

Photography: Jack Cox

Production: British International Pictures

89 mins.

Cast: Edmund Gwenn, Jill Esmond, John Longden

1932

Rich and Strange

Screenplay: Alma Reville, Val Valentine. Based on a theme by Dale Collins

Photography: Jack Cox, Charles Martin

Production: British International Pictures

87 mins.

Cast: Henry Kendall, Joan Barry, Percy Marmont

Number Seventeen

Screenplay: Alma Reville, Alfred Hitchcock, Rodney Ackland. Based on the play and novel by Jefferson Farjeon

Photography: Jack Cox

Production: British International Pictures

65 mins.

Cast: Leon M. Lion, Anne Grey, John Stuart, Donald Calthrop

1933

Waltzes from Vienna

Screenplay: Alma Reville, Guy Bolton. Based on a play by Dr. A. M. Willner, Heinz Reichert, and Ernst Marischka

Production: Tom Arnold

80 mins.

Cast: Jessie Matthews, Esmond Knight, Frank Vesper, Edmund Gwenn

1934

The Man Who Knew Too Much

Screenplay: A. R. Rawlinson, Edwin Greenwood. Based on an original subject by Charles Bennett and D. B. Wyndham-Lewis

Photography: Curt Courant

Production: Gaumont British

85 mins.

Cast: Leslie Banks, Edna Best, Nova Pilbeam, Peter Lorre

1935

The 39 Steps

Screenplay: Charles Bennett, Ian Hay. Based on the novel by John Buchan

Photography: Bernard Knowles

Production: Gaumont British

81 mins.

Cast: Robert Donat, Madeleine Carroll, Lucie Mannheim, Godfrey
Tearle, Peggy Ashcroft

1936

The Secret Agent

Screenplay: Charles Bennett, Ian Hay. Based on a play by Campbell
Dixon. Adapted from *Ashenden* by W. Somerset Maugham

Photography: Bernard Knowles

Production: Gaumont British

83 mins.

Cast: Madeleine Carroll, John Gielgud, Peter Lorre, Robert Young

Sabotage

Screenplay: Charles Bennett, Alma Reville, Ian Hay. Based on the
novel *The Secret Agent* by Joseph Conrad

Photography: Bernard Knowles

Production: Gaumont British

77 mins.

Cast: Sylvia Sidney, Oscar Homolka, John Loder, Desmond Tester

1937

Young and Innocent

Screenplay: Charles Bennett, Alma Revile. Based on a novel by
Josephine Tey

Photography: Bernard Knowles

Production: Gainsborough

80 mins.

Cast: Nova Pilbeam, Derrick de Marney, Percy Marmont

1938

The Lady Vanishes

Screenplay: Sidney Gilliat, Frank Launder. Based on the novel *The
Wheel Spins* by Ethel Lina White

Photography: Jack Cox

Production: Gainsborough

97 mins.

Cast: Margaret Lockwood, Michael Redgrave, Paul Lukas, Dame May Whitty

1939

Jamaica Inn

Screenplay: Sidney Gilliat, Joan Harrison. Based on the novel by Daphne du Maurier

Photography: Harry Stradling, Bernard Knowles

Production: Mayflower Pictures

100 mins.

Cast: Charles Laughton, Maureen O'Hara, Leslie Banks

1940

Rebecca

Screenplay: Robert E. Sherwood, Joan Harrison. Based on the novel by Daphne du Maurier

Photography: George Barnes

Art director: Lyle Wheeler

Editor: Hal C. Kern

Music: Franz Waxman

Producer: David O. Selznick

Production: Selznick International Release: United Artists

130 mins.

Cast: Laurence Olivier (Max de Winter), Joan Fontaine (Mrs. de Winter), George Sanders (Jack Favell), Judith Anderson (Mrs. Danvers), Nigel Bruce (Major Giles Lacey), C. Aubrey Smith, Reginald Denny, Gladys Cooper

Foreign Correspondent

Screenplay: Charles Bennett, Joan Harrison

Photography: Rudolph Mate

Art directors: William Cameron Menzies, Alexander Golitzen

Editors: Otho Lovering, Dorothy Spencer

Music: Alfred Newman

Producer: Walter Wanger

Production/release: United Artists

120 mins.

Cast: Joel McCrea (Johnny Jones), Laraine Day (Carol Fisher), Herbert Marshall (Stephen Fisher), George Sanders (Scott ffoliott), Albert Basserman (Van Meer), Robert Benchley (Stebbins), Eduardo Cianelli, Edmund Gwenn, Harry Davenport

1941

Mr. and Mrs. Smith

Screenplay: Norman Krasna. Based on an original story by Krasna

Photography: Harry Stradling

Art directors: Van Nest Polglase, L. P. Williams

Editor: William Hamilton

Music: Roy Webb

Producer: Harry E. Edington

Production/release: RKO

95 mins.

Cast: Carole Lombard (Ann Smith), Robert Montgomery (David Smith), Gene Raymond (Jeff Custer), Jack Carson (Chuck), Philip Merivak, Lucile Watson, William Tracy, Charles Halton

Suspicion

Screenplay: Samson Raphaelson, Joan Harrison, Alma Reville. Based on the novel *Before the Fact* by Francis Iles

Photography: Harry Stradling

Art director: Van Nest Polglase

Editor: William Hamilton

Music: Franz Waxman

Production/release: RKO

99 mins.

Cast: Cary Grant (John Aysgarth), Joan Fontaine (Lina NcLaidlaw), Nigel Bruce (Beaky), Sir Cedric Hardwicke (Gen. McLaidlaw), Dame May Whitty, Isabel Jeans

1942

Saboteur

Screenplay: Peter Viertel, Joan Harrison, Dorothy Parker. Based on an original idea by Hitchcock

Photography: Joseph Valentine

Art directors: Jack Otterson, Robert Boyle

Editor: Otto Ludwig

Music: Charles Previn, Frank Skinner

Producer: Frank Lloyd

Production/release: Universal

109 mins.

Cast: Robert Cummings (Barry Kane), Priscilla Lane (Patricia Martin), Otto Kruger (Tobin), Norman Lloyd (Fry), Alan Baxter, Alma Kruger, Vaughn Glazer, Dorothy Peterson

1943

Shadow of a Doubt

Screenplay: Thornton Wilder, Alma Reville, Sally Benson. Based on a story by Gordon McDonnell

Photography: Joseph Valentine

Art directors: John B. Goodman, Robert Boyle

Editor: Milton Carruth

Music: Dimitri Tiomkin

Producer: Jack H. Skirball

Production/release: Universal

108 mins.

Cast: Joseph Cotten (Charlie Oakley), Teresa Wright (Charlie Newton), MacDonald Carey (Jack Graham), Patricia Collinge

(Emma Newton), Henry Travers (Joseph Newton), Hume
Cronyn (Herb), Wallace Ford

Lifeboat

Screenplay: Jo Swerling. Based on a story by John Steinbeck

Photography: Glen MacWilliams

Art directors: James Basevi, Maurice Ransford

Editor: Dorothy Spencer

Music: Hugo Friedhofer

Producer: Kenneth MacGowan

Production/release: 20th Century-Fox

96 mins.

Cast: Tallulah Bankhead (Constance Porter), William Bendix (Gus
Smith), Walter Slezak (Willie), Mary Anderson (Alice), John
Hodiak (Kovac), Henry Hull (Charles Rittenhaus), Heather
Angel, Hume Cronyn, Canada Lee

1944

Bon Voyage

Screenplay: J.O.C. Orton, Angus MacPhail. Based on an original
idea by Arthur Calder-Marshall

Photography: Gunther Krampf

Art director: Charles Gilbert

Production: British Ministry of Information

35 mins.

Cast: John Blythe, the Moliere Players

Aventure Malgache

Photography: Gunther Krampf

Art director: Charles Gilbert

Production: British Ministry of Information

40 mins.

Cast: the Moliere Players

1945

Spellbound

Screenplay: Ben Hecht, Angus MacPhail. Based on the novel *The House of Dr. Edwardes* by Francis Beeding

Photography: George Barnes

Art directors: James Basevi, John Ewing. Dream sequences designed by Salvador Dali

Editors: William Ziegler, Hal C. Kern

Music: Miklos Rozsa

Producer: David O. Selznick

Production: Selznick International

Release: United Artists

110 mins.

Cast: Ingrid Bergman (Dr. Constance Peterson), Gregory Peck (John Ballantine), Leo G. Carroll (Dr. Murchison), Michael Chekov, Jean Acker, Rhonda Fleming, Donald Curtis, John Emery, Norman Lloyd

1946

Notorious

Screenplay: Ben Hecht. Based on a theme by Hitchcock

Photography: Ted Tetzlaff

Art directors: Albert S. D'Agostino, Carroll Clark

Editor: Theron Warth

Music: Roy Webb

Producer: Alfred Hitchcock

Production/release: RKO

100 mins.

Cast: Ingrid Bergman (Alicia Huberman), Cary Grant (Devlin), Claude Rains (Alexander Sebastian), Louis Calhern (Paul Prescott), Madame Konstantin (Mrs. Sebastian), Reinhold Schunzel (Dr. Anderson), Moroni Olsen, Ivan Triesault, Alex Minotis

1947

The Parading Case

Screenplay: David O. Selznick. Based on a novel by Robert Hichens, adapted by Alma Reville

Photography: Lee Garmes

Art directors: MacMillan Johnson, Thomas N. Morahan

Editors: Hal C. Kern, John Faure

Music: Franz Waxman

Producer: David O. Selznick

Production: Selznick International

132 mins.

Cast: Gregory Peck (Anthony Keane), Ann Todd (Gay Keane), Charles Laughton (Judge Horfield), Ethel Barrymore (Lady Sophie Horfield), Charles Coburn (Sir Simon Flaquer), Louis Jourdan (Andre Latour), Alida Valli (Mrs. Paradine), Leo G. Carroll

1948

Rope

Screenplay: Arthur Laurents. Based on the play by Patrick Hamilton, adapted by Hume Cronyn

Photography (Technicolor): Joseph Valentine, William V. Skall

Art director: Perry Ferguson

Editor: William H. Ziegler

Music: Leo F. Forbstein, based on Poulenc's *Perpetual Movement No. 1*

Producer: Hitchcock, Sidney Bernstein

Production: Transatlantic Pictures

Release: Warner Bros.

80 mins.

Cast: James Stewart (Ruport Cadell), Farley Granger (Philip), John Dall (Brandon), Joan Chandler (Janet Walker), Sir Cedric Hardwicke (Mr. Kentley), Constance Collier (Mrs. Atwater), Edith Evanson, Douglas Dick, Dick Hogan

1949

Under Capricorn

Screenplay: James Bridie. Based on the novel by Helen Simpson, adapted by Hume Cronyn

Photography (Technicolor): Jack Cardiff

Art director: Thomas N. Morahan

Editor: A. S. Bates

Music: Richard Adinsell

Producer: Hitchcock, Sidney Bernstein

Production: Transatlantic Pictures

Release: Warner Bros.

118 mins.

Cast: Ingrid Bergman (Lady Henrietta Flusky), Joseph Cotten (Sam Flusky), Michael Wilding (Charles Adare), Margaret Leighton (Milly), Jack Walling (Winter), Cecil Parker (the Governor), Dennis O'Dea (Corrigan), Olive Sloane

1951

Stage Fright

Screenplay: Whitfield Cook. Based on a novel by Selwyn Jepson, adapted by Alma Reville

Photography: Wilkie Cooper

Art director: Terence Verity

Editor: Edward Jarvis

Music: Leighton Lucas

Producer: Alfred Hitchcock

Production/release: Warner Bros.

110 mins.

Cast: Marlene Dietrich (Charlotte Inwood), Jane Wyman (Eve Gill), Michael Wilding (Inspector Wilfred Smith), Richard Todd (Jonathan Cooper), Alastair Sim (Commodore Gill), Sybil Thorndike (Mrs. Gill)

Strangers on a Train

Screenplay: Raymond Chandler, Czenzi Ormonde. Based on the novel by Patricia Highsmith, adapted by Whitfield Cook

Photography: Robert Burks

Art directors: Edward S. Haworth, George James Hopkins

Editor: William H. Ziegler

Music: Dimitri Tiomkin

Producer: Alfred Hitchcock

Production/release: Warner Bros.

100 mins.

Cast: Farley Granger (Guy Haines), Ruth Roman (Anne Morton), Robert Walker (Bruno Anthony), Leo G. Carroll (Sen. Morton), Patricia Hitchcock (Barbara Morton), Laura Elliott (Miriam Haines), Marion Lorne (Mrs. Anthony)

1952

I Confess

Screenplay: George Tabori, William Archibald. Based on a play by Paul Anthelme

Photography: Robert Burks

Art director: Edward S. Haworth

Editor: Rudi Fehr

Music: Dimitri Tiomkin

Producer: Alfred Hitchcock

Production/release: Warner Bros.

95 mins.

Cast: Montgomery Clift (Father Michael Logan), Anne Baxter (Ruth Grandfort), Karl Malden (Inspector Larrue), Brian Aherne (Willy Robertson), O. E. Hasse (Otto Keller), Dolly Hass (Alma Keller), Roger Dann (Pierre Grandfort)

1954

Dial M for Murder

Screenplay: Frederick Knott. Based on the play by Knott

Photography (Warnercolor, 3-D): Robert Burks

Art director: Edward Carrere

Editor: Rudi Fehr

Music: Dimitri Tiomkin

Producer: Alfred Hitchcock

Production/release: Warner Bros.

123 mins.

Cast: Ray Milland (Tony Wendice), Grace Kelly (Margot Wendice), Robert Cummings (Mark Halliday), John Williams (Inspector Hubbard), Anthony Dawson (Captain Lesgate)

Rear Window

Screenplay: John Michael Hayes. Based on a short story by Cornell Woolrich

Photography (Technicolor): Robert Burks

Art directors: Hal Pereira, Joseph MacMillan Johnson

Editor: George Tomasini

Music: Franz Waxman

Producer: Alfred Hitchcock

Production/release: Paramount

112 mins.

Cast: James Stewart (L. B. Jefferies), Grace Kelly (Lisa Fremont), Wendell Corey (Doyle), Thelma Ritter (Stella), Raymond Burr (Lars Thorwald), Judith Evelyn (Miss Lonely Hearts), Ross Bagdasarian (Song Writer), Georgine Darcy (Miss Torso), Jesslyn Fax (Miss Hearing Aid), Rand Harper (Honeymooner), Irene Winston (Mrs. Thorwald)

1955

To Catch a Thief

Screenplay: John Michael Hayes. Based on the novel by David Dodge

Photography (Technicolor, VistaVision): Robert Burks

Art directors: Hal Pereira, Joseph MacMillan Johnson

Editor: George Tomasini

Music: Lyn Murray

Producer: Alfred Hitchcock

Production/release: Paramount

97 mins.

Cast: Cary Grant (John Robie), Grace Kelly (Frances Stevens), Charles Vanel (Bertani), Jessie Royce Landis (Mrs. Stevens), Brigitte Auber, René Blancard, John Williams, Georgette Anys

1956

The Man Who Knew Too Much

Screenplay: John Michael Hayes, Angus MacPhail. Based on a story by Charles Bennett and D. B. Wyndham-Lewis

Photography (Technicolor, VistaVision): Robert Burks

Art directors: Hal Pereira, Henry Bumstead

Editor: George Tomasini

Music: Bernard Herrmann

Lyrics: Jay Livingston, Ray Evans. "Storm Cloud" cantata by Arthur Benjamin, D. B. Wyndham-Lewis

Producer: Alfred Hitchcock

Production/release: Paramount

119 mins.

Cast: James Stewart (Dr. Ben McKenna), Doris Day (Jo McKenna), Daniel Gelin (Louis Barnard), Brenda de Banzie (Mrs. Drayton), Bernard Miles (Mr. Drayton), Christopher Olsen, Ralph Truman, Mogens Wieth, Alan Mowbray

The Trouble with Harry

Screenplay: John Michael Hayes. Based on the novel by John Trevor Story

Photography (Technicolor, VistaVision): Robert Burks

Art directors: Hal Pereira, John Goodman

Editor: Alma Macrorie

Music: Bernard Herrmann

Producer: Alfred Hitchcock

Production/release: Paramount

99 mins.

Cast: Edmund Gwenn (Captain Wiles), John Forsythe (Sam Marlowe), Shirley MacLaine (Jennifer), Mildred Natwick (Miss Gravely), Jerry Mathers (Arnie), Mildred Dunnock (Mrs. Wit), Royal Dano

1957

The Wrong Man

Screenplay: Maxwell Anderson, Angus McPhail. Based on *The True Story of Christopher Emmanuel Balestrero* by Maxwell Anderson

Photography: Robert Burks

Art director: Paul Sylbert

Editor: George Tomasini

Music: Bernard Herrmann

Producer: Alfred Hitchcock

Production/release: Warner Bros.

105 mins.

Cast: Henry Fonda (Christopher Emmanuel Balestrero), Vera Miles (Rose Balestrero), Anthony Quale (O'Conner), Harold J. Stone, Charles Cooper, John Heldabrand

1958

Vertigo

Screenplay: Alec Coppel, Samuel Taylor. Based on the novel *D'Entre les Morts* by Boileau and Narcejac

Photography (Technicolor, VistaVision): Robert Burks

Art directors: Hal Pereira, Henry Bumstead

Editor: George Tomasini

Music: Bernard Herrmann

Producer: Alfred Hitchcock

Production/release: Paramount

128 mins.

Cast: James Stewart (John "Scottie" Ferguson), Kim Novak (Madeleine Elster, Judy Barton), Barbara Bel Geddes (Midge), Tom Helmore (Gavin Elster), Henry Jones (The Coroner), Raymond Bailey, Ellen Corby

1959

North by Northwest

Screenplay: Ernest Lehman

Photography (Technicolor, VistaVision): Robert Burks

Art directors: Robert Boyle, William A. Horning, Merrill Pye

Editor: George Tomasini

Music: Bernard Herrmann

Producer: Alfred Hitchcock

Production/release: MGM

136 mins.

Cast: Cary Grant (Roger Thornhill), Eva Marie Saint (Eve Kendall), James Mason (Phillip Vandamm), Jessie Royce Landis (Clara Thornhill), Leo G. Carroll (The Professor), Philip Ober, Josephine Hutchinson, Martin Landau

1960

Psycho

Screenplay: Joseph Stefano. Based on the novel by Robert Bloch

Photography: John L. Russell

Art directors: Joseph Hurley, Robert Clatworthy

Editor: George Tomasini

Music: Bernard Herrmann

Producer: Alfred Hitchcock

Production/release: Paramount

110 mins.

Cast: Janet Leigh (Marion Crane), Anthony Perkins (Norman Bates), Vera Miles (Lila Crane), John Gavin (Sam Loomis), Martin Balsam (Arbogast), John McIntire (Sheriff), Simon

Oakland, Frank Albertson, Patricia Hitchcock, Vaughn Taylor, Lurene Tuttle

1963

The Birds

Screenplay: Evan Hunter. Based on the story by Daphne du Maurier

Photography (Technicolor): Robert Burks

Art director: Robert Boyle

Editor: George Tomasini

Sound Consultant: Bernard Herrmann

Producer: Alfred Hitchcock

Production/release: Universal

120 mins.

Cast: Rod Taylor (Mitch Brenner), "Tippi" Hedren (Melanie Daniels), Jessica Tandy (Mrs. Brenner), Suzanne Pleshette (Annie Hayworth), Veronica Cartwright (Cathy Brenner), Ethel Griffies, Charles McGraw

1964

Marnie

Screenplay: Jay Presson Allen. Based on the novel by Winston Graham

Photography (Technicolor): Robert Burks

Art director: Robert Boyle

Editor: George Tomasini

Music: Bernard Herrmann

Producer: Alfred Hitchcock

Production/release: Universal

130 mins.

Cast: "Tippi" Hedren (Marnie Edgar), Sean Connery (Mark Rutland), Diane Baker (Lil Mainwaring), Martin Gabel (Strutt), Louise Latham (Bernice Edgar), Bob Sweeney, Alan Napier

1966

Torn Curtain

Screenplay: Brian Moore

Photography (Technicolor): John F. Warren

Art director: Frank Arrigo

Editor: Bud Hoffman

Music: John Addison

Producer: Alfred Hitchcock

Production/release: Universal

128 mins.

Cast: Paul Newman (Michael Armstrong), Julie Andrews (Sarah Sherman), Lila Kedrova (Countess Kuchinska), Wolfgang Kieling (Hermann Gromek), Hansjoerg Felmy, Tamara Toumanova, David Opatoshu

1969

Topaz

Screenplay: Samuel Taylor. Based on the novel by Leon Uris

Photography (Technicolor): Jack Hildyard

Art director: Henry Bumstead

Editor: William H. Ziegler

Music: Maurice Jarre

Producer: Alfred Hitchcock

Production/release: Universal

125 mins.

Cast: Frederick Stafford (Andre Devereaux), Dany Robin (Nicole Devereraux), John Forsythe (Michael Nordstrom), John Vernon (Rico Parra), Karin Dor (Juanita), Michel Piccoli (Jacques Granville), Philippe Noiret (Henri Jarre), Roscoe Lee Browne

1972

Frenzy

Screenplay: Anthony Shaffer. Based on the novel *Goodbye Piccadilly, Farewell Leicester Square* by Arthur La Bern

Photography (Technicolor): Gil Taylor

Production design: Syd Cain

Art director: Robert Laing

Editor: John Jympson

Music: Ron Goodwin

Producer: Alfred Hitchcock

Production/release: Universal

116 mins.

Cast: Jon Finch (Richard Blaney), Alec McCowen (Inspector Oxford), Barry Foster (Bob Rusk), Barbara Leigh-Hunt (Brenda Blaney), Anna Massey (Babs Milligan), Vivien Merchant (Mrs. Oxford), Bernard Cribbins, Billie Whitelaw

1976

Family Plot

Screenplay: Ernest Lehman. Based on the novel *The Rainbird Pattern* by Victor Canning

Photography (Technicolor): Leonard J. South

Production design: Henry Bumstead

Editor: J. Terry Williams

Music: John Williams

Producer: Alfred Hitchcock

Production/release: Universal

120 mins.

Cast: Bruce Dern (Lumley), Barbara Harris (Blanche), Karen Black (Fran), William Devane (Adamson), Cathleen Nesbitt (Julia Rainbird), Ed Lauter, Katherine Helmond, Nicholas Colasanto, William Prince

Reviews of *Rear Window,* 1954

REAR WINDOW

BOSLEY CROWTHER

New York Times, August 5, 1954. Reprinted with permission of the *New York Times.*

The boorish but fascinating pastime of peeking into other people's homes – a thing that New York apartment dwellers have a slight disposition to do – is used by Director Alfred Hitchcock to impel a tense and exciting exercise in his new melodrama, "Rear Window," which opened last night at the Rivoli.

Setting his camera and James Stewart in an open casement that looks out upon the backyards and opposite buildings of a jumbled residential block of lower Fifth Avenue *[sic],* the old thrill-billy has let the two discover a tingling lot about the neighbors' goings-on, including what appears to be a grisly murder by a sullen salesman across the way.

Mr. Hitchcock is nobody's greenhorn. When he takes on a stunt of this sort – and stunt it is, beyond question, not dissimilar from his more restricted "Rope" – he may be counted on to pull it with a maximum of build-up to the punch – a maximum of carefully tricked deception and incidents to divert and amuse.

This time he does it with precision. He and the writer of his script, John Michael Hayes, have concocted what might aptly be described as a "Street Scene" of middle-class content, viewed from the back instead of the front. The major observer of high drama – the fellow whom Mr. Stewart plays – is a world-roving news photographer who is confined to a wheelchair for the moment by a broken leg. And his rear-window observations range from two sun-bathing girls on a roof to the unseen but grimly indicated death of the salesman's wife.

The old master scans his action shrewdly. A glimpse of a ballet dancer here, stretching herself and spinning briskly about her apartment in scanty attire; a look there into the cluttered warren of a discouraged pianist, then, slyly, an inkling of the salesman's mysterious pursuit. Back in the apartment of the hero, he casually and cleverly suggests a bit of a personal involvement with a lovely, determined girl. And again, the glance of the camera ranges the rear-window view.

Mr. Hitchcock's film is not significant. What it has to say about people and human nature is superficial and glib. But it does exposes many facets of the loneliness of city life and it tacitly demonstrates the impulse of morbid curiosity. The purpose of it is sensation, and that it generally provides in the colorfulness of its detail and in the flood of menace toward the end.

The performances are in keeping. Mr. Stewart does a first-class job, playing the whole thing from a wheel chair and making points with his expressions and eyes. His handling of a lens-hound's paraphernalia in scanning the action across the way is very important to the color and fascination of the film.

Grace Kelly as the beautiful model who loves him and joins in the game of spying on a likely killer is fascinating, too. Thelma Ritter as a nurse who drops in daily; Wendell Corey as a dull professional sleuth, and Raymond Burr as the unsuspecting salesman, who is spied upon, perform with simple skill.

As in "Dial M for Murder," Mr. Hitchcock uses color dramatically. Without any gory demonstrations, he strongly suggests the stain of blood. In the polychromes seen from a rear window on steaming hot summer days and nights, and in the jangle and lilt of neighborhood music, he hints of passions, lust, tawdriness, and hope.

REAR WINDOW

BROG

Variety, July 14, 1954. Reprinted with permission of Variety, Inc. © 1998.

A tight suspense show with a bright boxoffice outlook is offered in "Rear Window," one of Alfred Hitchcock's better thrillers. James Stewart's established star value, plus the newer potentiality of Grace Kelly, currently getting a big build-up, and strong word-of-mouth possibilities indicate sturdy grossing chances in the keys and elsewhere.

Hitchcock combines technical and artistic skills in a manner that makes this an unusually good piece of murder mystery entertainment. A sound story by Cornell Woolrich and a cleverly dialoged screenplay by John Michael Hayes provide the producer-director with a solid basis for thrill-making. Of equal importance in delivering tense melodrama are the Technicolor camera work by Robert Burks and the apartment-courtyard setting executed by Hal Pereira and Joseph MacMillan Johnson.

Hitchcock confines all of the action to this single setting and draws the nerves to the snapping point in developing the thriller phases of the plot. He is just as skilled in making use of lighter touches in either dialog or situation to relieve this tension when it nears the unbearable. Interest never wavers during the 112 minutes of footage.

Stewart plays a news photographer confined to his apartment with a broken leg. He passes the long hours by playing peeping-tom on the people who live in the other apartments overlooking the courtyard. It's a hot, humid summer so shades are rarely drawn to block his view of intimate goings-on. In one of the apartments occupied by Raymond Burr and his invalid, shrewish wife Stewart observes things that lead him to believe Burr has murdered and dismembered the wife.

From then on suspense tightens as Stewart tries to convince Wendell Corey, a policeman buddy, his suspicions are correct. Already sold on the idea are Miss Kelly, Stewart's girl, and Thelma Ritter, the insurance nurse who comes daily to tend his needs.

With their help, Stewart is eventually able to prove his point, and almost gets himself killed doing it. Adding to the grip the melodrama has on the audience is the fact that virtually every scene is one that could only be viewed from Stewart's wheelchair, with the other apartment dwellers seen in pantomime action through the photog's binoculars or the telescopic lens from his camera.

There's a very earthy quality to the relationship between Stewart and Miss Kelly. She's a Park Avenue girl not above using all her physical charms to convince Stewart they should get married. This is carried to the point where she arrives one evening set to spend the night and gives him what she calmly calls "a preview of coming attractions" by donning frilly nightgown and negligee. Both do a fine job of the picture's acting demands.

Types that one might find in a Greenwich Village apartment add interest. Miss Torso, roundly played by Georgine Darcy, is a peeping-tom's delight, particularly when she loses her strapless bra. There is a great sadness to Miss Lonely Hearts, played by Judith Evelyn, a woman with an overwhelming desire for a man, yet not knowing what to do when she coaxes one in from the streets. There's a honeymoon joke in the actions of newlyweds Rand Harper and Harris Davenport. He's seen raising the shade at intervals, only to be called back to her arms by the bride. Ross Bagdasarian, a composer; Sara Berner and Frank Cady, a couple with a little dog; and the other types glimpsed all seem like real people, and their soundless contributions give the principals top-notch support. Burr is very good as the menace, as are Corey and Miss Ritter.

The production makes clever use of natural sounds and noises throughout, with not even the good score by Franz Waxman being permitted to intrude unnaturally into the drama.

THE CURRENT CINEMA: HITCHCOCK CONFINED AGAIN

JOHN McCARTEN

New Yorker, August 7, 1954. Reprinted by permission; © 1954 The New Yorker Magazine, Inc. All rights reserved.

The hero of the movie called "Rear Window" is a photographer who is firmly convinced that lens-and-shutter work is just about as fascinating an occupation as any man could dream of. When we encounter him, he is laid up with a broken leg in a Greenwich Village apartment. The apartment opens onto a court-yard full of people who lead singularly public lives, and our man, possibly because of the habit pattern induced by his calling, whiles away his immobile hours with a spot of voyeurism. At all hours of the day and night he keeps his neighbors under scrutiny through the lens of a telescopic camera of some sort, and becomes so intent about it that he barely has time to observe the power-fully attractive configurations of a young lady who visits him per-sistently, with high hopes that he will eventually reveal a compan-ionable spirit. When she broaches the idea of a permanent union, though, he bridles. "Did you ever eat fish heads and rice?" he demands. "Could you go through the jungle in high heels?" To this, the heroine, wearing a gown that must have cost her eleven hundred dollars, responds in the affirmative, but it gets her nowhere. "In my line of work, you don't sleep very much," the photographer goes on, "and sometimes the food you eat is made from things you couldn't look at alive."

No matter how upsetting the dietary notions of the cameraman may be, though, they are easier to take than the social notions of the neighbors he surveys so assiduously. One of these is a lady who gives cozy dinner parties for nonexistent guests; another is a dancer who leaps about incessantly; a third is a composer who attacks his piano with the stalwart fury of a lumberman trying to topple a redwood; and finally there is the villain of the piece – a Scandinavian gentleman presumably engaged in the lugubrious chore of butchering his wife. Although Peeping Tom spots this last one as something of a menace to society, a detective friend of his to whom he confides his suspicions insists that there is really no cause for alarm. After all, the detective points out, the fact that a man has several knives, a couple of fathoms of rope, an ominous-looking trunk, and a missing wife is no reason to jump to any hasty conclusions. Without going any further into the profes-sional logic of the detective, I will say "Rear Window" struggles heavily to make the point that an ounce of intuition on the part of a photographer is worth a pound of pragmatism on the part of a cop.

The author of this claptrap is Cornell Woolrich, a popular drugstore author, and Hollywood's affinity for him is easily under-standable. What isn't understandable, however, is Alfred Hitch-cock's association with this enterprise. He is billed as the director, and I fear that "Rear Window" must be taken as another example of his footless ambition to make a movie that stands absolutely still. In "Rope" and "Dial M for Murder," he worked, to all intents and purposes, in one room, and in the current foolishness, he is confined to an implausible back yard. Maybe one of these days he's going to bust out the way he used to, and then we'll have some satisfactory films. The cast Mr. Hitchcock has employed includes Thelma Ritter, at her indubitable best as a visiting nurse; James Stewart, as the photographer; Wendell Corey, as the opaque detective; and Grace Kelly, as Mr. Stewart's suitor. If it came to eat-ing fish heads and rice, I can't imagine anybody more likely to make them palatable than Miss Kelly. Indeed, her very presence in this film brings on an uncritical tolerance of the thing.

REAR WINDOW

STEVE SONDHEIM

Films in Review 5, No. 8 (October 1954). Reprinted with permission of *Films in Review*.

Alfred Hitchcock's *Rear Window* is his best picture in many years. It is more comic, though less sardonic, than *Strangers on a Train*, and in its characterization is as pointed as *Shadow of a Doubt*. It is less subtle than that masterwork, but has the same kind of serious moral undercurrent.

Rear Window tells the story of a grade A world-news photogra-pher (James Stewart) who, invalided with a broken leg, amuses himself by spying upon his Greenwich Village neighbors in the apartment building across the court. He sees what he thinks is a murder and sets out to prove it, and is almost killed for his pains.

Hitchcock and the screenwriter (John Michael Hayes) point out by implication the difference between civic responsibility and the feeling of power inherent in successful spying, and their story flows forward freely with but one flat statement of the film's premise – an impassioned speech to the world (the immediate neighbors) by an ex-vaudevillian *[sic]* on discovering that one of the tenants has killed her little dog.

Tension is almost non-existent in the first hour and a half of *Rear Window*, but the last twenty minutes are as exciting as anything Hitchcock has ever done. And what *Rear Window* lacks in suspense it more than makes up for in humor. Hitchcock's distinction as a director is not his ability to create suspense, as is commonly supposed. Other directors – Reed, Welles, Wyler – are equally adept with suspense. Hitchcock's brilliance is his wit, and his flawless technique for using that wit to support and counterpoint suspense. When his wit fails, his suspense fails (*I Confess, The Paradine Case, Under Capricorn, Rope*).

In *Rear Window* the dialogue is bright, but the direction is brighter still, as it needs to be, since so much of the action must be shown in half-seen, half-heard vignettes at a distance, and the camera must always be brought back to the immobilized Stewart.

Hitchcock gives us the essentials of a dozen lives with deft cinematic sureness. In about 30 seconds of screen time, e.g., he shows us the evolution of a quiet cocktail party into a cackling mob where everyone is having a good time except the host. We see, as a reflection on a window pane, Grace Kelly searching the murderer's apartment as the murderer enters his front door. The climactic fight is filmed almost entirely in close-up, which magnifies our sense of the invalid hero's immobilization, and resultant desperation.

Hitchcock's solution of how to take the spectator from Stewart to the apartments across the court and back again is ingenious and smooth. He does it by means of tracking shots from a specially designed boom. And since most of the action is shot from Stewart's point of view, Hitchcock makes sure the dialogue from across the court is audible but indistinct. The sounds are calculated to tease the listener in the way any barely overheard conversation does, and is very knowingly controlled.

A well-known Hitchcock trademark is his brief appearance in each of his films (in *Rear Window* he winds a clock in the composer's apartment). A less publicized but equally reliable trademark is the use of unusual effects in the climaxes of Hitchcock films (the Statue of Liberty sequence in *Saboteur*, the runaway carousel in *Strangers on a Train*, the single color shot in *Spellbound*). In *Rear Window* the hero makes a last-ditch defense against the murderer (Raymond Burr) by setting off flashbulbs in his face. Hitchcock photographs Burr's temporary blindness by means of a spectacular trick – an opening iris shot through color filters. The effect is surprising and visually powerful.

Not all of Hitchcock's devices are photographic. One of his best non-camera effects is suddenly running two suspense plots concurrently. As Miss Kelly searches the murderer's apartment, "Miss Lonelyhearts," on the floor beneath, contemplates suicide.

Stewart's performance could hardly be improved upon, and he even succeeds in projecting an almost old-maidish nosiness without losing audience sympathy. Thelma Ritter's dead-pan realism is well used in the part of a gore-happy nurse. Wendell Corey as the detective must suggest two opposed concepts simultaneously, and does so with skill. The other actors, who play mostly in pantomime, are able – Burr, Ross Bagdasarian, Sara Berner, and Judith Evelyn, despite the cliched bit of business of her opening pantomime (setting an intimate dinner for an imaginary man).

But *Rear Window*'s acting honors belong to Grace Kelly, who more than justifies the publicity build-up she's been getting. Beautiful, well-bred, exuding subdued sex, she blithely projects charm that is never pretentious and sophistication that is never phoney.

Rear Window is not without flaws, especially in the closing moments when all the incidental character subplots are quickly and tritely tied together. Toward the end ludicrous lyrics, sung offscreen to music which a composer in the film has been trying to write throughout the picture, illogically and most inappropriately refer to the character Miss Kelly plays. Half-way through *Rear Window* we are not certain there will be a murder, not sure that Hitchcock may not have a new gimmick, which is to let us *think* there'll be a murder.

This last, however, may not have been unintentional, since it is a most effective substitute for suspense.

Select Bibliography

BOOKS ON HITCHCOCK

Brill, Lesley. *The Hitchcock Romance: Love and Irony in Hitchcock's Films.* Princeton, NJ: Princeton University Press, 1988.

Cohen, Paula Merantz. *Alfred Hitchcock: The Legacy of Victorianism.* Lexington: University of Kentucky Press, 1995.

Corber, Robert. *In the Name of National Security: Hitchcock, Homophobia, and the Political Construction of Gender in Postwar America.* Durham, NC: Duke University Press, 1993.

Deutelbaum, Marshall, and Leland Poague, eds. *A Hitchcock Reader.* Ames: Iowa State University Press, 1986.

Durgnat, Raymond. *The Strange Case of Alfred Hitchcock.* Cambridge, MA: MIT Press, 1974.

Kapsis, Robert. *Hitchcock: The Making of a Reputation.* Chicago: University of Chicago Press, 1992.

LaValley, Albert J., ed. *Focus on Hitchcock.* Englewood Cliffs, NJ: Prentice-Hall, 1972.

Modleski, Tania. *The Women Who Knew Too Much: Hitchcock and Feminist Theory.* London and New York: Methuen, 1988.

Montcoffe, Francis. *Fenêtre sur cour, Alfred Hitchcock: Étude critique.* Paris: Nathan, 1990.

Raubicheck, Walter, and Walter Srebnick, eds. *Hitchcock's Rereleased Films: From Rope to Vertigo.* Detroit: Wayne State University Press, 1991.

Rohmer, Eric, and Claude Chabrol. *Hitchcock: The First Forty-Four Films.* New York: Ungar, 1979.

Rothman, William. *Hitchcock: The Murderous Gaze.* Cambridge, MA: Harvard University Press, 1982.

Sharff, Stefan. *The Art of Looking in Hitchcock's Rear Window.* New York: Limelight Editions, 1997.

Sloan, Jane E. *Alfred Hitchcock: The Definitive Filmography.* Los Angeles: University of California Press, 1993.

Spoto, Donald. *The Art of Alfred Hitchcock.* New York: Hopkinson and Blake, 1976.

The Dark Side of Genius: The Life of Alfred Hitchcock. Boston: Little, Brown, 1983.

Taylor, John Russell. *Hitch: The Life and Times of Alfred Hitchcock.* New York: Pantheon, 1978.

Truffaut, Francois. *Hitchcock.* New York: Simon and Schuster, 1967.

Weis, Elisabeth. *The Silent Scream: Alfred Hitchcock's Sound Track.* Rutherford, NJ: Farleigh Dickinson Press, 1982.

Wood, Robin. *Hitchcock's Films Revisited.* New York: Columbia University Press, 1989.

Hitchcock's Films, 3rd ed. New York: A. S. Barnes, 1977.

Zizek, Slavoj, ed. *Everything You Always Wanted to Know About Lacan (But Were Afraid to Ask Hitchcock).* London: Verso, 1992.

ARTICLES

Almansi, Renato J. "Alfred Hitchcock's Disappearing Women: A Study in Scopophilia and Object Loss," *The International Review of Psychoanalysis* 19, No. 1 (1992): 81–90.

Appel, Alfred, Jr. "The Eye of Knowledge: Voyeuristic Games in Film and Literature," *Film Comment* 9, No. 3 (May–June 1973): 20–6.

Atkinson, David. "Hitchcock's Techniques Tell *Rear Window* Story," *American Cinematographer* 71, No. 1 (January 1990): 34–40.

Belton, John. "The Space of *Rear Window,*" *Modern Language Notes* 103, No. 5 (December 1988): 1121–38.

Benton, Robert J. "Film as Dream: Alfred Hitchcock's *Rear Window,*" *Psychoanalytic Review* 71, No. 3 (November 1984): 483–500.

Bordwell, David. "The Viewer's Activity," *Narration in the Fiction Film.* Madison: University of Wisconsin Press, 1985.

Chion, Michel. "*Rear Window* d'Alfred Hitchcock: Le quatrieme coté," *Cahiers du Cinéma,* No. 356 (February 1984): 4–7.

Cohen, Steve. "*Rear Window:* The Untold Story," *Columbia Film View* 8, No. 1 (Winter/Spring 1990): 2–7.

"Setting the Record Straight: Screenwriter John Michael Hayes Talks About Hollywood and Hitchcock," *Columbia Film View* 8, No. 1 (Winter/Spring 1990): 8–13.

Douchet, Jean. "Hitch and His Public," *New York Film Bulletin* 7 (1961). Rep. in Deutelbaum and Poague.

Ferrara, Patricia. "Through Hitchcock's *Rear Window* Again," *New Orleans Review* 12, No. 3 (1985): 21–30.

Harris, Thomas. "*Rear Window* and *Blow-Up:* Hitchcock's Straight-for-wardness vs. Antonioni's Ambiguity," *Literature/Film Quarterly* 15, No. 1 (1987): 60–63.

Lee, Sander H. "Escape and Commitment in Hitchcock's *Rear Window*," *Post Script* 7, No. 2 (Winter 1988): 18–28.

Lewis, Matthew P. "Bringing Down the Curtain on *Rear Window*: Copyright Infringement and Derivative Motion Pictures," *Loyola Entertainment Law Journal* 10, No. 1 (1990): 237–60.

Mason, C. "*Rear Window*'s Lisa Freemont: Masochistic Female Spectator of Post-war Socio-economic Threat," *Florida State University Conference on Literature and Film* 16 (1991): 109–121.

Miller, Gabriel. "Beyond the Frame: Hitchcock, Art, and the Ideal," *Post Script* 5, No. 2 (Winter 1986): 31–46.

Mogg, Ken. "The Gioconda Smile: Archetypes in/of Hitchcock's *Rear Window* (1954)," *The MacGuffin* No. 23 (November 1997): 7–26.

Mulvey, Laura. "Visual Pleasure and Narrative Cinema," *Screen* 16, No. 3 (Autumn 1975): 6–18.

Naremore, James. "Film as Performance Text: *Rear Window*," in *Acting in the Cinema*. Berkeley: University of California Press, 1988.

Odabashion, B. "The Unspeakable Crime in Hitchcock's *Rear Window*: Hero as Lay Detective, Spectator as Lay Analyst," *Hitchcock Annual* (Fall 1993): 3–11.

Palmer, Barton R. "The Metafictional Hitchcock: The Experience of Viewing and the Viewing of Experience in *Rear Window* and *Psycho*," *Cinema Journal* 25, No. 2 (1986): 4–19.

Sered, Jean. "The Dark Side," *Armchair Detective* 22, Nos. 2–3 (Spring–Summer 1989): 116–135, 240–258.

Smith, J. "The Strange Case of Lars Thorwald: Rounding Up the Usual Suspect in *Rear Window*," *New Orleans Review* 19, No. 2 (1992): 21–9.

Staiger, Janet. "Toward a Historical Materialist Approach to Reception Studies," *Interpreting Films: Studies in the Historical Reception of American Cinema*. Princeton, NJ: Princeton University Press, 1992.

Stam, Robert, and Roberta Pearson. "Hitchcock's *Rear Window*: Reflexivity and the Critique of Voyeurism," *Enclitic* 7, No. 1 (Spring 1984): 136–145. Rep. in Deutelbaum and Poague.

Streich, Joseph L. "How TV Remakes the Classics," *Village Voice* (March 11, 1986): 43.

Toles, George E. "Alfred Hitchcock's *Rear Window* as Critical Allegory," *boundary 2* 16, Nos. 2–3 (Winter–Spring 1989): 225–246.

Wood, Robin. "Fear of Spying," *American Film* 9, No. 2 (November 1983): 28–35.

Woodcock, John M. "The Name Dropper: Alfred Hitchcock," *American Cinematographer* 40, Nos. 2–3 (Summer 1990): 36–37.

REVIEWS

Anon. "The New Pictures," *Time* 64 (August 2, 1954): 72–73.

Anon. "Peeping Tom Spots a Killer," *Life* 37, No. 7 (August 16, 1954): 88–90.

Anon. *"Rear Window," Catholic World* 179 (August 1954): 383.

Anon. *"Rear Window," Newsweek* 44 (August 9, 1954): 80–81.

Anon. *"Rear Window," Saturday Review* 37 (August 21, 1954): 31.

Anon. *"Rear Window," Look* 18 (September 21, 1954): 50–51.

Anon. *"Rear Window* Ruling Favors Woolrich Story Rights-Holder," *Variety* (January 4, 1989): 3.

Bornemann, Ernest. *"Rear Window," Films and Filming* 1, No. 2 (November 1954): 18.

Canby, Vincent. *"Rear Window* – Still a Joy," *New York Times* 133 (October 9, 1983): sec. 2, p. 21, col. 1.

Chabrol, Claude. "Les Choses Serious," *Cahiers du cinema* 8, No. 46 (April 1955): 41–43.

Crowther, Bosley. "Mr. Hitchcock Peeps: A *Rear Window* View Seen at the Rivoli," *New York Times* (August 5, 1954): 18.

  "A Point of View: Hitchcock's *Rear Window* Provokes Contrast of This and Other Films," *New York Times* (August 15, 1954): sec. 2, p. 1.

Gavin, Arthur. *"Rear Window," American Cinematographer* 35, No. 2 (February 1954): 76–78, 97.

Hartung, Philip T. "Look Now," *Commonweal* 60 (August 13, 1954): 463.

Hyams, Joe. "Hitchcock's *Rear Window,"* *New York Herald Tribune* (August 1, 1954).

May, Derwint. *"Rear Window," Sight and Sound* 24, No. 2 (October–December 1954): 89–90.

McCarten, John. "The Current Cinema: Hitchcock Confined Again," *New Yorker* 30 (August 7, 1954): 47.

Phillips, Louis. "Through a Glass Darkly: A Consideration of Alfred Hitchcock's *Rear Window," Armchair Detective* 18, No. 2 (Spring 1985): 190–193.

Rose, Lloyd. "Alfred Again," *Atlantic* 252, No. 4 (October 1983): 100–102.

Sarris, Andrew. "The Critical Anatomy of Alfred Hitchcock," *Village Voice* 28 (October 18, 1983): 57.

Sondheim, Steve. *"Rear Window," Films in Review* 5, No. 8 (October 1954): 427–429.

Zunzer, Jesse. "Hitchcock's Scariest in Years Comes to Town," *Cue* 7 (August 1954): 15.

Index